150 YEARS OF BRITISH RAILWAYS

Edited by Martin Hedges
Consultant editor Patrick Whitehouse

This edition published exclusively for W H Smith

Published by
The Hamlyn Publishing Group Limited
London · New York · Sydney · Toronto
Astronaut House
Hounslow Road
Feltham, Middlesex

Produced by
Basinghall Books Limited
59 Cambridge Road
Kings Heath, Birmingham

ISBN 0 600 37655 9

Printed in Hong Kong
by South China Printing Co.

CONTENTS

Just as railways have been in existence for over one hundred and fifty years so has literature apertaining to them – in fact some would say that there has been a plethora of such work in the last two decades alone. Both editors have recognised this fact and that there is little, if anything, new to say, but a celebration is, after all, a celebration and 1980 commemorates the birth of the public passenger train a century and a half ago. This, in itself was one of the biggest landmarks in the development of the industrial revolution assisting the changing of Britain from an agricultural country to an industrial one. Much was due to the rapid and cheap transit of both passengers and goods. Of course this romantic story has and will always have its special devotees but without the railway historian a great deal of intriguing fact could have been lost for ever and we would all be the poorer for it. Thus the editors would like to thank all those whose works they have consulted and in particular the renowned father and the erudite son, C. J. Allen and G. F. Allen who have, probably more than most, ensured that matters needing to be recorded have been duly set down, remembering too that as much railway history has been made during the last generation as in the previous one hundred and twenty years. E. L. Cornwell and G. Kichenside have done a great deal of the leg work for this book – a somewhat daunting task in the time set them and we are most grateful. Our thanks are also due to many photographers whose work appears in these pages and particularly to those dedicated amateurs who have photographed trains as their hobby – no true history can be presented without their pictures.

P.B.W.
M.H.

RAILWAYS ARE BORN

It is just a century and a half since the first railways, built specifically for carrying passengers and planned from the start for operation by steam locomotives, were opened to lay the foundations of the British railway system that we know today. The Liverpool & Manchester, and the Canterbury & Whitstable railways, both opened in 1830, confirmed the successful combination of the steam locomotive with the iron rail as a potent new form of transport which, within a decade, began to spread its tentacles not only across Britain but also into other parts of the world. Yet railways and steam power had originally developed independently and it was not until the early nineteenth century that the first real moves were made to bring them together.

The origin of the railway in the form of a guidance system for carts and wagons is lost in the mists of history. The Romans were known to have dug ruts in mountain roads to prevent wheeled vehicles from straying too close to the edge of the precipice. By the fifteenth century mines in central Europe had timber baulks to provide a smooth route over rough ground for the hand barrows of the miners; the system was later improved to include a guide pin running between baulks of timber to prevent the barrow wheels from running off the edges of the planks. Where larger horse-drawn wagons were used, a raised timber edge rail stopped wheels from leaving the running surface. Then wooden flanged wheels appeared which obviated the need for the guiding timbers, since the wheels would stay on the running timbers by the action of the flange.

By the early eighteenth century coal mining was becoming established in Britain, especially in the Tyneside area, and numerous wagonways were built from the mine exits to the river Tyne to carry coal down to the river for onward carriage by sea. In 1787 the invention by John Curr of the L-section iron plate rail completely transformed methods of transport underground. Its successful use in the mines quickly lead to its adoption on the surface for mineral wagon-

An early Tyneside wagonway – the beginning of railways for industrial use. A print from T H Hair's 'Views of the Collieries'. (British Museum)

9

Richard Trevithick's *Catch as Catch
Can* railway on demonstration in
Euston Square in 1809. From a
Science Museum print. (Colourviews
Picture Library)

ways in many parts of the country. It was an improvement on the use of iron plates to provide a more durable surface to wooden rails which had first been seen at Coalbrookdale in 1767. The next stage was the realisation that much freer running was gained by using an iron wheel on an iron rail. The consequent loss of friction – and therefore resistance – between wheel and rail meant that considerably heavier loads could be carried in a wagon and a horse was able to haul more than one vehicle. The addition of a metal flange to the wheel proved so successful that the metal flanged wheel superseded all other designs for the transportation of rolling stock over the iron rails. With the use of modern steel (and with the exception of localised urban trains with rubber tyres running on a concrete way as in Paris and elsewhere) it remains the standard railway principle throughout the world.

The harnessing of steam power was first allied closely to mining, though for the purpose of pumping out water rather than in a transport capacity. Mining was being carried on extensively in several parts of the country by the end of the eighteenth century, with the Cornish metal mines and the collieries of Durham and Northumberland ranking as the most important. In both these areas the mines had for almost a hundred years been taking advantage of steam-powered engines to work the pumps which extracted water from the deep workings. At this time, however, there was insufficient knowledge of the ideal combinations of materials and design techniques to take full advantage of the capabilities of steam and the pressures at which engines would work were seriously limited. The Newcomen engine, the first successful example of which was built to pump water near Dudley Castle in 1712, used steam not as a direct method of propulsion but to create a vacuum against which atmospheric pressure reacted to move a piston. The amount of steam required to produce the vacuum meant that the Newcomen engines were huge. They were also very slow running. James Watt improved the engine by enclosing both ends of the cylinder and making the piston double acting, but it was Richard Trevithick, a Cornishman, who designed a steam engine in which pressure of the steam was directly responsible for moving the piston, at the same time allowing the exhaust to discharge into the atmosphere rather than condense. The harnessing of steam at high pressure thus became possible and much more power could be generated from a cylinder of a given size. Now it became conceivable for a vehicle to be constructed which would propel itself by the use of high pressure steam on a piston head and which would also have sufficient power to haul an additional load. The steam locomotive engine was almost in sight.

After a number of pioneers had tried to build such a machine in the late eighteenth century, Trevithick constructed a road locomotive in 1801 and two years later was closely involved in the design and building of what is now accepted as the first steam locomotive to be tried on rails – at Coalbrookdale ironworks. In 1804 his second steam locomotive hauled a ten-ton load over a distance of 9.5 miles in four hours at Pen-y-Darren Tramway, South Wales. Although the trial, which won a wager of 500 guineas, was successful, it presaged a problem which was to plague many a locomotive builder in the future: the weight of the engine was such that it broke the rails.

Thus it was not long before the 'locomotive' was demoted to function as a stationary engine powering a hammer at the ironworks – the purpose for which it was originally intended. Indeed, none of Trevithick's four locomotives was put to prolonged commercial rail use and even his last engine, built in 1808, which hauled passenger wagons round a small circular track as an entertainment near what is now the University of London at Euston, did not last long. Certainly at that time it did not inspire the imagination of anybody with what the potential of a steam railway might be.

The technical problem of supporting the weight of locomotives was to remain unsolved for several years. The cast-iron rails of the early railways could not sustain the shock imposed by the weight of passing trains for long, even after the introduction of the fish-bellied shape. Somehow the engine designers had to resolve the problem of building locomotives which could carry sufficient weight to gain the necessary grip between their iron wheels and the iron rails but were not so heavy that they damaged the track. Many of the horse-worked tramways and railways had been built along routes which included some fairly steep gradients and these presented additional problems of adhesion to the new steam locomotive. For a long time the designers could not find a solution to this weight-adhesion equation and instead concentrated on other means of providing extra grip between wheels and rail. The inventiveness of John Blenkinsop produced a combination of a rack with running rails which gave the Middleton Railway the first successful colliery locomotive in 1812.

A year later William Hedley demonstrated that it was, after all, possible to gain sufficient adhesion for the successful transmission of power through the carrying wheels. In that year his *Puffing Billy* and

Richard Trevithick's pioneer engine of 1803 hauled a train of 25 tons on the Pen-y-Darren tramway (South Wales) in February 1804. It ran on a flanged plateway. Subsequent locomotives to his design were tried out on the Wylam Wagonway in Northumberland on wooden rails. (Colourviews Picture Library)

George Stephenson, from the painting by John Lucas. (*The Illustrated London News*)

Early documents relating to the world's first public railway to use steam power, the Stockton & Darlington Railway which opened in 1825. (British Tourist Authority)

Wylam Dilly engines were put into service. However, though he had apparently solved the problem of slippage, both Hedley's locomotives were too heavy for the track and to spread the weight they were rebuilt to run on eight instead of four wheels. When stronger rails of wrought or rolled iron had been installed, they were re-converted back to four-wheelers and had a long working life. *Wylam Dilly*, which is now on exhibition at the Royal Scottish Museum in Edinburgh, continued to be used until 1866; *Puffing Billy* is exhibited at the Science Museum in South Kensington, London.

An avid observer of the work of the locomotive pioneers, George Stephenson was soon to emerge with his own ideas. Born in 1781 at Wylam, Newcastle-upon-Tyne, in a cottage beside the tramway, it was not unnatural that he should become involved with railways. This he did by taking employment as an assistant fireman at a local colliery. He became fascinated by the idea of overcoming some of the inherent problems of their operation through improving their design and in his early thirties he was appointed enginewright for a group of collieries in the Killingworth area. Here he was able to develop his own plans for steam locomotives and also to devote time to working out new principles of railway operation and construction.

Like all the early steam locomotive builders, Stephenson faced many design problems with his first engines. He overcame them by some features which gave the machines what would later be regarded as a cumbersome look. One problem to which he turned his attention was the loss of efficiency due to inadvertent condensation. Trevithick's principle of using high-pressure steam relied on there being no condensation either in the cylinder or in a separate condenser. To guard against loss of efficiency the Cornishman had placed the cylin-

ders inside the boiler. This, Stephenson also did but rather than siting
them at one end, as Trevithick had done, he simplified transmission
of thrust to the driving wheels by placing them in the top of the
boiler. Cross-beams on the tops of the long piston rods confined the
side thrusts during each revolution of the wheels to a relatively small
amount and this helped the primitive slide bars or parallel motion
arrangements to withstand the force. A basic system of springing
cushioned the locomotive to some extent against the shocks which
were inevitable from a rough and irregular permanent way and this,
by helping to cut out some jumping, improved adhesion between
wheels and rails. The springing also had the added benefit of reducing
shock and so prevented or at least cut down the number of rail breaks.

As Stephenson developed his work at Killingworth it was only
natural that his reputation as a locomotive engineer should spread
quickly, particularly as it was becoming obvious that collieries could
gain considerable advantages from using their own products to
provide the fuel for steam locomotives. Stephenson was asked to
build locomotives for other places. Of greater importance at this

The 1975-built full-sized replica of George Stephenson's *Locomotion* was on display at the 150th Anniversary celebrations of the Stockton & Darlington Railway at Shildon. (J Hunt)

stage, however, were the plans which he produced for a railway system to provide an outlet for the coal from Hetton Colliery near Sunderland, County Durham. His plans incorporated the use of locomotives or horses on gentle gradients, the employment of the 'falling weight' of loaded wagons descending to pull up empty wagons, or the use of stationary steam engines to haul wagons up inclines by rope. Each of these methods was used when the Hetton Colliery Railway was opened in November 1822. Today one of the original locomotives is preserved at Beamish Open Air Museum as part of the National Collection. In 1925 it had the honour of heading the spectacular procession of locomotives staged to mark the centenary of the Stockton & Darlington Railway.

Opened in 1825, the Stockton & Darlington was also designed to provide an outflow for colliery production, in this case the coal from the Auckland Coalfield which until then had been carried along an inadequate coal road. Proposals for this undertaking, which was even more ambitious than the Hetton Colliery Railway, had first been put forward publicly in 1810 and there had been much debate about the feasibility of the project. George Stephenson met one of the promoters of the scheme, Edward Pease, of Darlington, on the very day that the Act of Parliament granting permission for the railway was passed in 1822. Subsequently Stephenson was appointed engineer of the line and made a number of important changes to the original plans which improved the route and made its future operation considerably easier. It was he who proposed that the company should seek the necessary permission from Parliament for steam locomotives to be used.

Not surprisingly, it was George Stephenson's own 'improved locomotive engine' *Locomotion* which hauled the inaugural train to Stockton on 27 September 1825. It pulled 600 passengers in 38 wagons a distance of 21 miles from Shildon and reached a speed of 15mph. By the end of the following November the success of the new railway had been responsible for bringing down the price of coal in Stockton by one-third; within 18 months it was more than halved and the railway company was already making a profit.

Initially the freight wagons on the Stockton & Darlington were mostly hauled by horses, although it quickly became apparent that, despite their unreliability, locomotives were 30 per cent cheaper to operate.

All passenger traffic was horse-drawn for the first eight years of the railway's existence, this work being sub-let to contractors who used their own vehicles and paid a toll to use the company's line. In fact, the line could be used by anyone who paid the appropriate fee. The Stockton & Darlington Act had specified that the owners of land adjoining the line were entitled to build their own branch lines on their land if they wished. The idea of a public railway with open access and upon which anyone could use their own vehicle proved unfeasible since it was quickly appreciated that there had to be a high degree of discipline and co-ordination which could only be provided under one company. The Stockton & Darlington effectively heralded the arrival of the new style of railway company.

George Stephenson's *Locomotion* and its three sister engines were refined versions of his early colliery locomotive design but they were still unreliable and prone to quite frequent breakdowns. Even so, they compared favourably with the next to be delivered to the Stockton & Darlington, an engine which was nicknamed *Chittaprat* because of the noise it made. This was so prone to failures that it was soon taken out of service. However, its boiler shell was incorporated in the 0–6–0 *Royal George* built by Timothy Hackworth. This locomotive started operating in November 1827 and proved a far more successful machine. It was the first of the double-tender locomotives designed by Hackworth which were to become characteristic of the Stockton & Darlington. Two later engines of this design are preserved: *Samson* in New Glasgow, Nova Scotia, and *Derwent* at Darlington North Road Museum.

News of the success of the Stockton & Darlington spread quickly and it rapidly became an object of close study by many of those who wished to promote or build new railways. Stephenson's fame had spread still more rapidly and even before the S & D was opened he had been approached by the directors of the Liverpool & Manchester Railway. With the approval of the S & D directors, Stephenson

An old Hackworth locomotive at South Hetton Colliery 10 October 1947. (H C Casserley)

accepted an offer to become engineer of what was to be an even bigger project.

The Liverpool & Manchester Railway was the first to be designed from the outset to incorporate all the ingredients of an inter-city railway for freight and passengers. Previously, as we have seen, the first consideration had been the provision of good outlet routes for mining production. The importance of the L & MR scheme was that it would connect two major centres of industry and commerce, both of which were growing rapidly and could only become more important to the economic strength of the region. The existing, highly developed water transport system by river and canal was extremely well used and companies were paying annual dividends of 50 per cent and more. Railway speculators saw that the time was ripe for their new transport system to take a share of the profits and they set about turning the proposals – which had been talked about for several years – into reality.

When Stephenson took up his new appointment in May of 1824 he immediately put in hand route surveying so that the path of the necessary Parliamentary formalities could be smoothed by presentation of a route which could be seen to be feasible. In view of the strength of the water transport industry throughout Lancashire it was hardly surprising that the L & MR proposals met with considerable opposition from this direction or that water transport rates were cut by 25 per cent in advance of the railway opening to dissuade potential customers from switching their allegiance.

By the end of 1824 – before his Stockton & Darlington project was completed – Stephenson's survey of the L & MR route had been finished and the Bill was presented before Parliament. Now came a setback: work on the Bill had obviously been rushed and the opposition was quick to seize any gaps in the information and to have the Bill thrown out. It was to be another year before the company, having carried out another, fuller survey, saw the Act passed. In the meantime a good deal of behind-the-scenes dealing had gone on to buy off the opposition.

J Dixon's engraving shows the elevation and plan of the suspension bridge carrying the Stockton & Darlington Railway over the river Tees near Stockton. (Durham County Library)

The final line of the Liverpool & Manchester was chosen to make it the most economic route possible and rather than make unnecessary detours to avoid obstacles, thousands of labourers were brought in to remove the obstacles themselves. It must be remembered and appreciated that civil engineering was still in the infancy of mechanisation; some of the engineering work carried out on this first inter-city line was breathtaking in its size and daring. A cutting 70ft deep, Olive Mount, was hewn out of solid rock; a superb viaduct of nine arches carried the double track over the Sankey Valley; and the rails were laid across the uneasy surface of Chat Moss.

The directors of the L & MR were determined to find the best locomotive to operate their new line and though many had been built after the opening of the Stockton & Darlington, none of them had proved outstanding and unreliability was still a problem. To seek out the best the directors organised a competition, the famous 'Rainhill Trials', in October 1829. This was not a race and competitors had to observe stringent regulations. Each locomotive had to travel 37.5 miles twice – representing the return trip between Liverpool and Manchester – with an allowance for getting up speed. However the distance was not covered in two straight journeys but by the locomotives' travelling backwards and forwards over the

1.75-mile course on Rainhill level, hauling a load. On the first day about 15,000 sightseers watched the trials and public interest continued unabated throughout the trials.

Stephenson had entered his new *Rocket*, an engine which was a considerable improvement on the earlier *Locomotion*. It was *Rocket* that emerged as the eventual winner of the £500 prize, having shown that it was more than equal to the requirements of the trials. *Rocket*'s leading wheels were rotated by short connecting rods braced to the outside cylinders by simple slide bars, thereby dispensing with the overhead beams of colliery locomotives. This new arrangement provided greatly improved efficiency in the use of the steam which was now produced in a multi-tube boiler fitted with an external firebox surrounded by a water jacket. Exhaust steam was emitted through a blast pipe, providing automatic regulation of the fire draught and, therefore, of the rate of steam generation. Indeed, *Rocket* was the first locomotive to incorporate, albeit in fairly simple form, the principal features necessary to propel a machine by steam successfully and economically.

Rocket was, of course, one of the locomotives chosen to take part in the celebrations which were staged to mark the opening of the Liverpool & Manchester Railway on 15 September 1830. Eight special trains carried dignitaries and the common people from Liverpool to Manchester. The guest of honour was the prime minister, the Duke of Wellington, and it was his train which was in the first recorded fatality involving a passenger train. As it stood at Parkside to take on water, William Huskisson, the Liverpool MP and President of the Board of Trade, left the prime minister's carriage and was crushed between the side of it and the *Rocket*, which was hauling a train on the adjacent track. He was seriously injured and rushed by a train (hauled by *Northumbria* and driven by Stephenson himself) to hospital in Eccles, where he died that night.

The L & MR quickly became a commercial success and outstripped the Stockton & Darlington and other companies by using steam locomotives to haul all its trains. Stockton & Darlington continued to use horses for some freight and the other contractors we have previously mentioned also used horses for passenger operations. The L & MR attracted passenger and freight because of its 'all-steam' image and as a result other transport undertakings suffered; for example, more than half the stagecoaches which had worked between Liverpool and Manchester were off the road within three months. By the end of 1830 the L & MR was able to report a net profit of £14,432 on just three and one-half months' operation. The age of the passenger-carrying steam railway had arrived.

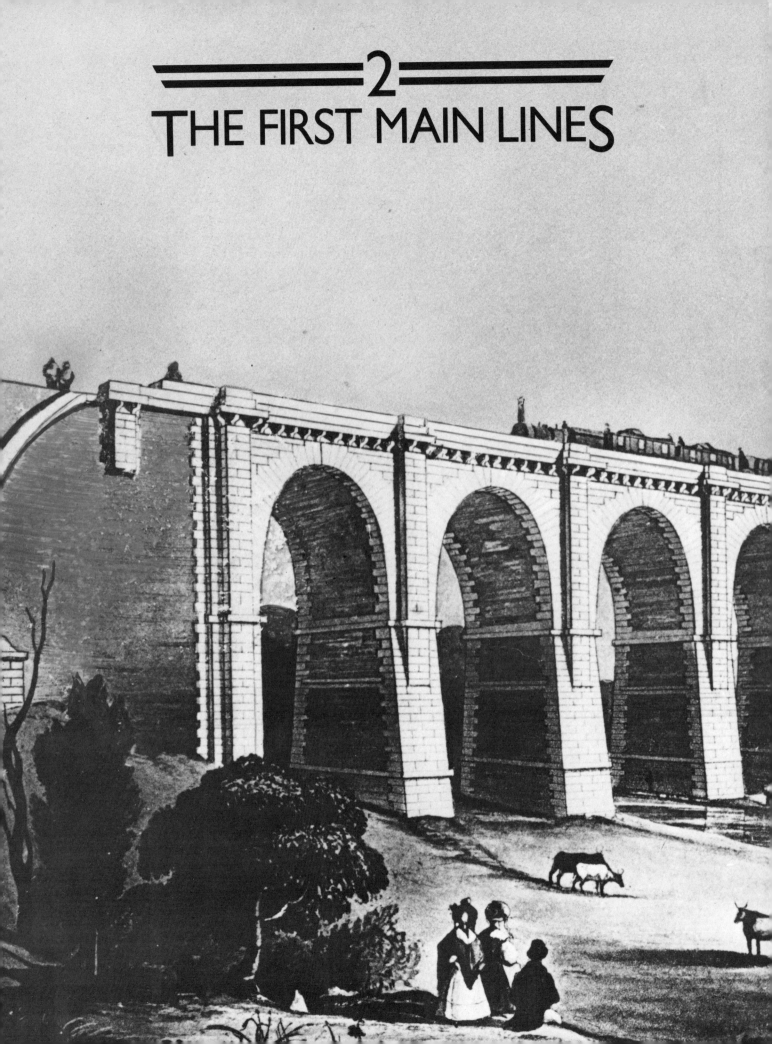

2
THE FIRST MAIN LINES

The first public passenger railway –
a scene on the Liverpool &
Manchester Railway, drawn by
Ackerman, shows a train on the
Sankey Viaduct. (National Railway
Museum)

Within five years of the opening of the Stockton & Darlington
Railway the role of the railway in Britain was changing. Instead of
being regarded merely as a short-haul transport system primarily of
benefit to industry, it was seen as the primary means of moving people
as well as freight between major cities.

While many powerful individuals and lobbies remained against the
railways and fought hard to keep the builders away, others were
equally determined that any proposed line should be built in such a
way as to serve all the major towns near the projected route. More
often than not their proposals were not only uneconomic but also
doomed to failure because of topographical problems. The construction, for example, of a railway over the 112 miles from London to
Birmingham was a far more complicated and costly operation than
building 31 miles of line from Liverpool to Manchester.

The London & Birmingham Railway, opened in 1837–38, was the
first trunk main line from London. Its construction presented new
civil engineering problems involving deep cuttings, inclines and
tunnels. The line had to climb the Chiltern hills and the Northamp-
tonshire hills and cross the rivers Avon, Ouse and Thames. George
Stephenson's son, Robert, who was to be regarded by many as the
greatest engineer of the era, was appointed chief engineer. He plotted
the route to include gentle curves and easy gradients which involved
major engineering and construction works such as the Watford and
Kilsby tunnels, the deep cuttings at Tring and Roade and the long
viaduct at Wolverton. Fortunately, Robert Stephenson had not
only been given an excellent formal education – which his father

An early photograph of the Liverpool & Manchester Railway locomotive *Rocket* before it was rebuilt. (Colourviews Picture Library)

top:
The famous Doric-arch entrance to old Euston station was demolished in the mid-1960s to make way for the new terminus. (National Railway Museum)

could afford thanks to his own success – but had also gained valuable practical experience of railway building by working with George on the Stockton & Darlington and later in North America. He was perhaps the most influential of all railway engineers and his Britannia Tubular Bridge over the Menai Strait – one of the two great bridges he designed – has been described as the greatest and boldest civil engineering feat of the early Victorian era. (His second bridge, the Royal Border at Berwick, completed a direct Anglo-Scottish east coast route in 1850.)

The southern terminus of the London & Birmingham was Euston station, which was able to claim that it was the gateway to the north because from there it was possible to reach both Liverpool and Manchester via Birmingham. This came about because the L & B's northern terminus, Curzon Street, in Birmingham, was shared with the Grand Junction Railway which linked Birmingham with those two northern cities. With the completion during the next decade of lines from Birmingham to Derby, York and beyond, Euston was the only station in the capital to serve the north. It retained this distinction until 1850, when Maiden Lane, just north of today's Kings Cross, was opened in London with the new main line to Peterborough, Doncaster and York.

Not unnaturally the ports of the south of England attracted the attention of railway builders since there was an obvious demand to link them with London. The London & Southampton was opened in stages beginning in 1837 but Southampton was then far from being the great port it is today. In fact, it was the coming of the railway and

The cutting at Mornington Crescent, 1836, a sketch by J C Bourne of the building of the London & Birmingham Railway. (National Railway Museum)

right:
Excavation work for the building of the London & Birmingham Railway at Park Village, Camden, 26 August 1836. Sketch by J C Bourne. (National Railway Museum)

the development of steamships which allowed Southampton to expand.

Of far greater commercial importance at the time was the city of Bristol, which was still regarded as England's second city in the early 1820s and had a thriving port. The building of the Great Western Railway from Bristol to London was therefore of major significance and the line lived up to expectations. It was superbly planned and executed, with curves and gradients reduced to the minimum by

Grand Junction Railway's Vauxhall
station, Birmingham, 1838.
(Colourviews Picture Library)

Isambard Kingdom Brunel. It was he, also, who selected the unique
gauge for the GWR of 7ft 0¼in, firmly believing that this was the
ideal, though it was to present problems later. From the first, though,
it set the GWR apart from other companies as doing things differently.

The gauge of the Stockton & Darlington was 4ft 8in. It would be
nice to accept the folklore which says that Stephenson chose this after
surveying the axle widths of road carts; in fact the gauge was already
in use on the wagonways of the north-east. Stephenson saw no
reason to change the gauge on which he had carried out some of his
early experiments when it was laid on the Killingworth lines. He had
used the same gauge on the Hetton Colliery Railway and did so
again on the Liverpool & Manchester. It was, of course, to become
the standard gauge, though the extra half-inch (to 4ft 8½in) was
allowed later to give better clearance between the reverse of the
wheel flanges and the check rails. (Today standard gauge is 4ft 8⅜in,
the small adjustment having been made to reduce the tendency of
bogies to 'hunt' or vibrate laterally at high speeds.)

It was Brunel who introduced the continuous beam timber
sleepers for his broad-gauge track. Previously, the iron rails had been
laid separately on wooden or stone blocks in parallel rows, with
stone blocks supporting the ends of each length of rail. While there
were advantages to Brunel's 'baulk road' – the beams gave continuous
support and held the track more accurately to its gauge – it also
provided a very rough ride since it reduced the vertical give of the
rail at a time when there was only a minimum of springing in rolling
stock. Despite this, Brunel persisted with the continuous beam until
the end of broad gauge, even though other companies had adopted
the transverse beam system still followed today. Indeed the greatest
advantage of Brunel's 'baulk road' was in the ease with which it
could be removed when the GWR finally completed its changeover
to standard gauge in May 1892 by converting the track west of
Exeter in just two days!

A poster of 1838 outlines the penalties for theft. (Colourviews Picture Library)

Apart from other considerations, the broad gauge created problems because it was incompatible with standard gauge. This meant that when the lines of the GWR met those of other companies there could be no easy sharing arrangement as occurred elsewhere. Such was the extent of concern over the 'battle of the gauges' as it has become known, that Parliament set up a Gauge Commission to investigate each system. When the Commissioners visited Gloucester to witness the transfer of Bristol and Gloucester Railway freight from one system to the other they saw a scene of total chaos and delay. On the other hand, though totally unimpressed with the transfer arrangements, the Commission did come down in favour of the performance of broad-gauge locomotives over those of narrow-gauge. However, that was not enough to stop them from recommending that in future all railways should be built to the standard gauge. Opposition by the GWR to the Gauge Bill made it less restrictive than it might have been and even after it became law, railway companies were able to specify exemption from standard gauge. Broad gauge could still be used for lines built in areas already covered by the GWR. The peak of broad gauge was in the mid-1860s, when 1040 miles of broad and 387 miles of mixed gauge had been laid from London to Weymouth, Penzance, New Milford and Wolverhampton. Even so, inroads had been made by standard gauge into this territory, whose borders were also surrounded by 4ft 8½in tracks.

Brunel was nothing if not an innovator and he adopted an unusual method of propulsion for the South Devon Railway's extensions through the county – the use of the atmospheric system. Though the line was, like other continuations of the broad-gauge system, built by a separate company, the GWR had a considerable financial interest in it, as a major shareholder and as part-owner of the Bristol and Exeter Railway. Brunel was also its engineer.

Atmospheric or pneumatic propulsion had been patented by Clegg and Samuda in 1839 and had been used on the Dublin and Kingstown Railway and also between Croydon and Epsom. The system proposed for South Devon, where it was thought that it would give easier working over the steep gradients around Dartmoor and would cut costs, involved the installation of a 15in diameter pipe between the track. A piston was attached to the leading vehicle through a slot in the top of the pipe, the slot being closed in front of the piston attachment by means of a continuous flexible flap over which a small wheel ran to make a seal behind the piston. It was then possible to exhaust the air from the pipe ahead of the piston by means of stationary pumping engines. Atmospheric pressure entered the pipe behind the piston and forced it through the tube; the train thus was pushed along.

After initial trials in the spring of 1847, the system came into public use between Exeter and Teignmouth in September. Though there were occasional mishaps and delays, the system won universal support and gave a smooth ride and a clean journey. However, complications soon arose, particularly with the leather seal. Not only did it prove to be a popular meal for wayside rats, the leather was porous and was almost permanently saturated or, in winter, frozen stiff. In addition, corrosion set in between the tannin and the fastenings. Less than a year after its public inception, the atmospheric

Early days on the Great Western:
J C Bourne's sketch of the pioneering
days of the 7ft 0¼in gauge:
The engine house at Swindon.
(Colourviews Picture Library)

pressure system was useless, the whole of the leather valve from Exeter to Newton Abbot having disintegrated. Faced with repairs which would cost £250,000 and the knowledge that operating costs were higher than had been estimated, the company ceased to use this method of propulsion. The subsequent sale of plant raised a mere £43,000 – a tenth of the capital cost.

Undoubtedly George Stephenson, who had dismissed the method as 'a great humbug', gained some degree of satisfaction from its failure. Nevertheless, Brunel's purpose in decreeing its adoption had been to try a new form of propulsion which could have saved some of the great cost of earthworks and tunnelling involved in trunk-route construction. The fact that the system passed its initial trials was sufficient justification for Brunel to go ahead; the presence of some excessively steep gradients in South Devon are a permanent reminder that in the end he was proved wrong.

Among those who sprang to fame as a result of the new railway age was Thomas Brassey, perhaps the pre-eminent railway contractor, who undertook the building of 1700 route miles in Britain (plus 2800 miles abroad). When Joseph Locke was working on the construction of the London and Southampton Railway, Brassey secured contracts worth £4.3 million to build 118 miles of the line. While working on the Grand Junction Railway, Locke, incidentally, had devised a system of estimating that worked well where a small force of contractors was involved. Brassey's labour force went beyond the 'small' and at one time numbered 45,000 men working in Britain and on the continent. Indeed, British railway builders spread their influence and their labour forces wide: Brassey engineered lines from Paris to Rouen, Le Havre, Nantes and Cherbourg and in Holland and Spain; Brunel surveyed lines between Florence and Pistoia and from Genoa to Alessandria in Italy; Robert Stephenson worked in Belgium, Sweden and Switzerland.

The conditions under which the workmen lived and worked on the new lines were often appalling. Shanty towns were built in the depth of the countryside while, if construction work was being carried out near towns, only the meanest of hovels and most primitive sanitary facilities were provided. The result was that death, disease and injury were commonplace. Opposite York station a burial ground was opened in 1832 for the victims of a cholera epidemic. In the six years required to build the line over the Pennine range more than 100 bodies were taken for burial at Chapel-le-Dale and others were interred near the mouth of Blea Moor Tunnel. Workmen were killed or maimed not only in major disasters such as tunnels collapsing or flooding but also in relatively simple operations. To survive, the men had to be tough and fearless and accidents often occurred when they were showing off their prowess or after drinking orgies which followed fortnightly pay-days. The men were, incidentally, known as 'navvies', a name derived from the 'navigators' who laboured to build Britain's navigable waterways a century before.

Though by no means causing death or disease, the conditions under which second- and third-class passengers travelled were also extremely primitive. They rode in open wagons, some with seats and some without, and had to suffer the smoke and cinders as well as the extremes of the British climate. By contrast, first-class travel was luxurious: passengers rode in covered coaches with a degree of furnishing and upholstery and even oil or candle lights in some coaches. The compartments in a coach derived from the builders' intention to make the carriages as much like a terrace of stage-coaches as possible.

In fact it was possible for road travellers to take to the railways without changing carriages: the road carriages were loaded on to flat railway wagons. This was a sensible marketing idea which proved an added attraction in drawing passengers away from conventional means of road travel. The greatest advantage which the railways had, however, was that they were able to convey passengers more quickly to their destinations.

In 1835 coaching was at its peak with 3300 stage-coaches and 700 mail coaches on the roads each day. However, the Post Office had begun using the railways to transport mail on the Liverpool & Manchester as early as 1830. The introduction of stamps and the penny post by Rowland Hill in 1840 saw the railways poised to carry the flood of mail which was to follow.

When the seal of royal approval was set upon the new form of passenger transport, travel by rail became more than a convenience; it was the correct 'modern' thing to do. In 1839 Prince Albert, who was returning from a visit to Queen Victoria at Windsor, travelled on the GWR from Slough to Paddington. It was three years before the Queen herself was persuaded to journey by rail from Windsor to London but in 1840 Queen Adelaide, widow of William IV, became the first queen to use this mode of transport.

By 1842 far more passengers were using the railways than the stage-coaches. In addition, with a network of nearly 2000 miles of tracks, the railway companies were generating new freight traffic as well as continuing to attract custom away from the waterways. The framework of the main rail trunk system was laid and in operation, the people had taken to steam locomotion for themselves and their goods, and the companies were profitable with an annual revenue of about £4 million.

The curtain was about to be raised on the most dramatic period of railway construction and speculation which would see the trunk send out branches to cover the length and breadth of the country.

Goods shed at Bristol by J C Bourne.
(Colourviews Picture Library)

3
THE 'MANIA' YEARS

The Stockton and Darlington Railway Company's authorised capital when the act allowing its construction was passed in 1821 was just over £100,000 for a route of almost 27 miles, or rather less than £4000 a mile. That act had been the twenty-first passed in Britain since the start of the century to authorise a railway to be built. By the mid-1840s Parliament was coping with a rush of such bills seeking enactment and the cost of railway construction had risen dramatically.

Total authorised capital for the whole country aggregated about £76 million for a route mileage of just over 4000 – or about £19,000 a mile. (In fact by the beginning of 1845 only 2150 miles of line had been opened to traffic.) Yet the tidal wave of new construction against which these figures become mere droplets was still to come. By the spring of the following year there were no less than 519 railway bills awaiting Parliamentary approval, involving a total share capital of around £230 million.

The railway mania had, of course, been set off by the success of some, if not all of the early companies and by the fact that there were still many areas of the country ripe for railway development. The attraction was not generally altruistic; it lay in the chance for personal prestige and fortune for those who could launch successful companies and actually see their railway operating.

Virtually every railway scheme had to have Parliamentary approval and there were various standing orders which had to be observed in an attempt to exclude all but *bona fide* applicants. Because of the queue of bills awaiting approval, attempts were made to shorten the procedure in the House of Commons but even so the presentation of each bill gave its opponents a chance to raise all kinds of objections to its contents or the likely consequences if it was passed. In particular, there was opposition from those speaking on behalf of existing railway companies which felt their own interests might be damaged by a new company in opposition.

Even after the Acts had been passed the opposition to new lines did not always stop. Apart from deliberate attempts to prevent the new companies raising the necessary capital, there were also ways of delaying the construction work itself once it got under way. Fights between navvies and gangs of 'roughs' raised by the opposition occurred quite often.

In the 1840s company accountancy was a generally haphazard affair and the companies were required only to account to their shareholders – and even then in broad detail. There was no obligation to present detailed financial accounts to Parliament, the Board of Trade or the public. It was easy enough, anyway, to conceal details of, for example, expenditure from the revenue account by lumping it under the heading of 'capital', thereby apparently increasing the profitability of an operation and, where possible, enabling dividends to be paid out of capital. Railway companies could conceal their shaky foundations well enough to be able to continue attracting shareholders' support and new investment.

Nor was it difficult to rig the stock-market value of shares in the railway companies by forcing prices up or down artificially through bulk buying or selling of shares. There was nothing to prevent

The Royal Albert Bridge, Saltash, joins Devon and Cornwall. Built in 1859 it was considered Brunel's last victory. From *The London Illustrated News*. (Colourviews Picture Library)

dubious characters from floating a new railway company and selling shares in it without any intention of proceeding with the flamboyant plans which had been used to attract buyers' attention. The company could simply be allowed to die or be traded off after the dubious entrepreneurs had creamed off their share of the 'profits', the investors being left with nothing. Today it seems extraordinary that in 1836 four different schemes were put before Parliament for companies to operate between London and Brighton; all were unsuccessful yet in the next Parliamentary session six more schemes were promoted.

An indication of the way in which the 'railway-rush' of the 1840s developed comes from the fact that in 1843 24 Acts were passed to permit new lines to be built; in the successive three Parliamentary sessions thereafter the number of bills presented rose to 37, then 248 and finally to 815. Over 700 of these reached the Private Bills Office, the others failing to be considered for a variety of reasons.

From 1845 to 1847 Parliament sanctioned 8592 route miles in three sessions, yet little more than one-third of that total was actually built; the balance of about 5500 miles was either abandoned or quietly forgotten.

Fortunately, despite the highly suspect nature of many of the railway companies of this period, there were those who saw to it that reputable railway construction continued. Once London was linked with north-west England, the next natural objective became Scotland. The Wigan branch of the Liverpool & Manchester had

The Chepstow tubular suspension bridge and the junction of the Severn and the Wye Rivers, 1852. From *The Illustrated London News.* (Colourviews Picture Library)

Kings Cross station train shed 1851.
From *The Illustrated London News.*
(Colourviews Picture Library)

been opened in 1832 as a small step further north and in 1838 the Northern Union Railway went beyond Wigan to Preston. Two years later came the opening of the Lancaster & Preston Railway. From Lancaster the road mail coaches for Carlisle, Edinburgh and Glasgow were now timed to connect with the trains. In August of 1840, two months after this development, the Glasgow & South Western Railway opened its first section, which connected the city with Ardrossan. Previously the day mail trains between London and Liverpool had connected with the Liverpool-Ardrossan steamer; now the mail could go all the way by rail.

That year saw other important route developments. Through trains were introduced from London Euston to York, following the London & Birmingham Railway's line to Rugby and then taking the Midland Counties Railway route through Leicester to Derby. From there the route was over North Midland tracks to Altofts Junction. The northward advance was furthered by the opening of the Preston and Wyre Railway's line to the port of Fleetwood, from where the Ardrossan steamer service operated thereafter.

The important step, though, was from Lancaster, over the Westmorland fells to Carlisle. George Stephenson was not entirely happy about a route he had supported across Morecambe Bay from Hest Bank to Kents Bank on an embankment and thence to Ulverston, Millom and Whitehaven. Joseph Locke carried out independent surveys and selected a route almost due north from Lancaster over the 915ft high Shap Fells, preferring to climb the heights rather than tunnel on grounds of cost. The challenge of this long haul was one which was important not only to civil engineers building the line but also to those who had to design the locomotives to traverse it. Today's electrically powered trains from the south barely slacken pace up the last 1-in-75, four-mile climb and even have to reduce power to remain within the 75mph speed limit but to the steam locomotives of the 1840s the climb was a trudge. The line from Lancaster to Oxenholme, near Kendal, was opened in September 1846 and at the same time the Oxenholme to Kendal and Windermere line went into operation. Three months later the Shap section of the Lancaster and Carlisle Railway was opened.

The first continuous rail links between Scotland's two principal cities (Edinburgh and Glasgow) and London were forged by the opening of the Caledonian Railway's Beattock to Carlisle section in September 1847 and the Beattock to Glasgow and Edinburgh in February 1848.

On the East Coast route to Scotland a temporary bridge was opened over the Tyne in October 1848. Robert Stephenson's High Level Bridge at Newcastle-upon-Tyne was completed in 1849 and with the opening of his Royal Border Bridge at Berwick in 1850 the East Coast route was vastly improved. Trains still run to and from Euston via Rugby and thence over the various lines controlled by George Hudson, an entrepreneur from the Midlands, northwards to Berwick.

Hudson, a native of York, was one of the first to exploit the railways in the pursuit of personal power, prestige and fortune. His business life had started with a drapery shop but a legacy of £30,000 enabled him to buy his way into the world of railway finance. A tough individualist, he had the money and soon bought the influence which opened up the corridors of power to him and found him seats on the boards of companies. His toughness made him ideal as a 'trouble-shooter' and soon he was attaining company chairmanships as well as the office of Lord Mayor of York in 1837 and he became a Member of Parliament for Sunderland in 1845. One of his chairmanships was of the York and North Midland which had been formed to link York with the London to Leeds lines at Altofts Junction. Not content with this, Hudson went on to lease the Leeds and Selby Railway in 1840. He thereupon removed most of its passenger services so that travellers were forced to go via Methley and his own York and North Midland.

Having secured control of railway traffic between the West Riding and York and Humberside, Hudson went on to increase his power by promoting schemes to extend the Great North of England from Darlington to Newcastle. He hoped to reach agreement with the Stockton and Darlington for a line-sharing arrangement but failed and so drove his line at right angles through the S & D at Darlington. This strange flat 'junction' of the two lines lasted well into this century.

It was Hudson who secured for the North British Railway the right to build the line from Edinburgh to Berwick. Thereafter, completion of the two Robert Stephenson bridges we have mentioned over the Tweed and Tyne, completed the East Coast link between London and Scotland. Not content with his undoubted power in his native northlands, however, Hudson also gained the

The Royal Border Bridge at Berwick-on-Tweed, designed by Robert Stephenson took a little over three years to build. From *The Illustrated London News*. (Colourviews Picture Library)

support of shareholders of the North Midland (as opposed to the York & North Midland) and they voted him into the chairmanship.

In 1844 he was the prime mover of the amalgamation of the North Midland, the Midland Counties and the Birmingham & Derby Junction into the Midland Railway. All three of these railways met at Derby and NM had been in furious competition with the Midland Counties and the Birmingham & Derby to attract customers for through passage to London. As an example of the fare-cutting, the 38-mile journey from Derby to Hampton-in-Arden cost only one shilling (5p).

Though Hudson's motives can be questioned in a number of his dealings, it has to be admitted that others were to be of considerable benefit to company shareholders. His successful appeals to investors in those three companies to sink their differences was an example of this. It also, of course, gave him rule over routes extending from Bristol and Rugby to Edinburgh! Not for nothing was he known as the Railway King.

However, his reign was nearing its end. The existing rail route from London Euston to York ran mainly over lines which he controlled. Not surprisingly he therefore bitterly opposed proposals for a direct line from London to York. This time, though, he was over-ruled and the Great Northern Railway gained permission to open a route from Askern, near Doncaster, to London via Retford, Lincoln, Boston and Peterborough. Between Askern and York the company used the tracks of the Lancashire & Yorkshire Railway to Knottingley, where there was a junction with the York & North Midland. The London terminus at Maiden Lane was a temporary one. It served from August 1850 until October 1852, when Kings Cross was brought into use following completion in August of the direct line from Peterborough to Retford. In the interim a detour had been made via Lincoln.

The fact that it was possible for the Great Northern to reach York over one of the lines controlled by Hudson – the York & North Midland – was an indication of his diminishing power. The great railway-rush was slowing and the value of railway shares had fallen. As always in such circumstances, questions were then raised about Hudson's management of the finances of various companies and in 1849 shareholders of the Eastern Counties Railway vocally chastised him. Next it was discovered that the value of shares in his companies had been maintained by paying dividends out of capital. In April Hudson resigned his chairmanship of the Midland Railway and a subsequent committee of inquiry found that the Railway King had 'abused the confidence that was placed in him by wielding the power he obtained to forward his own interest'. Nevertheless, Hudson had made an undoubted contribution to the establishment of a viable railway system and he has a just memorial in Hudson House, British Rail's Eastern Region headquarters in York.

Parliament had always shown a preference for a larger number of companies competing against each other but Hudson's successful amalgamation to form the Midland Railway broke this pattern. The Grand Junction Railway took over the Liverpool & Manchester in 1845 and in the following year the London and North Western Railway was formed by the amalgamation of the Grand Junction, London & Birmingham and the Manchester & Birmingham, opened only four years previously between Manchester and Crewe. (Birmingham was reached over Grand Junction tracks.)

The Grand Junction took with it into the new company – destined to become the largest stock company in the world – some of the sections of the West Coast route to Scotland, north of the Liverpool & Manchester line. In 1859 the Lancaster and Preston Junction and the Lancaster and Carlisle Railways were leased to the LNWR and were vested in that company in 1879.

A similar process of acquisition and amalgamation led to the formation in 1854 of the North Eastern Railway to establish a major company for the East Coast route. The main constituents of the NER were the York, Newcastle & Berwick, the York & North Midland and the Leeds Northern.

Parliament continued to exercise control over the formation of new railway companies, which still required an Act. Though there had been disquiet over the size of the new LNWR it had eventually been granted the necessary Act. However, when the Midland Railway later wanted to amalgamate or 'co-operate' with the LNWR and sought Parliamentary approval in 1869, it was refused. Instead the

Britannia Bridge, built in 1850, was Robert Stephenson's masterpiece of tubular construction linking Anglesey with the mainland. From *The Illustrated London News*. (Colourviews Picture Library)

Midland approached the Great Northern, which agreed that its trains could use Kings Cross as its London terminus, running in on the line from Hitchin. This resulted in proposals for a Midland/Great Northern merger, but again Parliament opposed the idea, which was dropped.

Even so, acquisition and mergers continued among the small companies to set the pattern for Britain's railway system which was to remain almost unchanged until the 'Grouping' of companies after World War I. Whereas the Industrial Revolution was started in some countries by the emergence of the railways, in Britain it was the railways which accelerated the revolution and fed upon the expanding markets which it had provided for travel and transport of freight.

The railways were quick to see the advantages of cheap return tickets, particularly at holiday periods which had now established a new pattern of movement by the populace to the expanding 'holiday resorts'. Since trains on which cheap fares were obtainable were frequently overcrowded, it was a natural development for firms or organisations to want to reserve complete trains for their members. The pioneer in this new market for the chartered train was Thomas Cook with his special train from Leicester to Loughborough which took a party of about 1000 temperance reformers on an excursion on 5 July 1841. Cheap tickets to the Continent were first offered by the South Eastern Railway in 1848 and Thomas Cook began organising Continental holidays in 1855.

The Great Exhibition at the Crystal Palace in Hyde Park, London in 1851 prompted one of the first large-scale organised movements of passengers by rail. One-million people a month visited the exhibition during the six months it was open and they travelled to London

LOST

On the Rail Road between Preston and Birmingham, on Friday, 9th of September,

A LARGE

PORTMANTEAU,

of Black Leather, with a Painted Cover, marked in white letters "*G. Puzzi*," and on the Portmanteau itself a Brass Plate engraved "*G. Puzzi*," containing a white leather Portfolio, with Trinkets and Jewellery, and a variety of Papers; also a large quantity of Wearing Apparel and Linen marked with the initials "G. P." Also the amount of 150 New Sovereigns, and a quantity of Silver, the amount not exactly known. Among the Trinkets was a large Gold Seal, marked with a double "P."

Whoever will give information of the above loss to Mr. WALTER, 56, Davies Street, Berkeley Square, London, that will lead to the recovery of the Property—or if Stolen, the conviction of the Offender or Offenders—shall be most handsomely Rewarded.

Sept: 15, 1842.   London : Wm. Davy, Printer, Gilbert-st., Oxford-st.

An 1842 wall poster from the early London & North Western Railway. (Colourviews Picture Library)

very largely by train from all parts of the country and from the sea ports whence they had arrived from overseas. Excursion fares were available for as little as five shillings (25p) return between Manchester or Leeds and London. For the International Exhibition in Paris in 1867 Cook arranged excursions for working men which cost only 34 shillings (£1.70) for four days.

Having at first treated third-class passengers as little more than cattle, the railways now did all they could to attract the working classes to take advantage of their concessionary fares. In 1844 they had been offended by Gladstone's Act which required them to run what became known as 'Parliamentary trains' with proper seating (wooden benches), protection from the weather and fares of not more than one penny a mile for third-class passengers. By the 1850s the companies realized that the policy of encouraging mass travel by offering cheap fares was paying dividends. In fact by 1880 third-class travel accounted for almost 38 per cent of receipts and a decade later the receipts exceeded those for first- and second-class tickets. Even so, little attempt was made to improve third-class accommodation until the middle of the 1870s when the Midland Railway led the way by introducing padded seats and proper compartments instead of shoulder-high wooden partitions. Even then, it was another 20 years before these improvements became widespread.

The companies attempted not only to attract the custom of the working classes on holiday, they also set about providing services to convey working people to and from their places of employment. The coming of railways to the towns had the effect of prompting many middle class families to move to the outskirts or even into more rural surroundings from where the head of the family would commute by train. The physical act of carving the rail routes into the towns also had another effect: much housing was demolished, particularly in working-class areas, and workmen who had previously lived close to their places of work had also to move further away and travel by train daily. The railway companies offered special cheap-rate workmen's trains which, in turn, encouraged the growth of new suburbs. More than this, the needs of railways themselves also led to the growth of 'railway towns' such as Swindon and Wolverton. The former was a small market town until the Great Western Railway chose it as the site for its locomotive and carriage works. By 1851 92 per cent of Swindon's population were employed in the railway workshops. Wolverton was chosen by the London & Birmingham Railway for its locomotive works because it was approximately mid-way along the line and was close to the Grand Junction Canal. By 1851 85 per cent of the population worked for the railway. Similarly other towns grew because they became railway junctions.

The railways were thus playing an important role in re-shaping the whole life of the country, socially, commercially, and even topographically.

4

QUEST FOR POWER

Despite the twenty-five years of pioneering development between Trevithick's first railway locomotive and the Rainhill trials in 1829, the shape of locomotives and the arrangement of essential components continued very much on a 'hit-or-miss' basis for several years after the trials.

George Stephenson's 'stable' of engines for the Stockton & Darlington which followed the *Rocket* were broadly similar but they did not have its high, steeply inclined cylinders. Instead, the cylinders were lowered and their angle altered so that they lay almost horizontally as it was thought that the original arrangement caused unsteady motion.

The first locomotive on which the cylinders were placed between the frames below the smokebox and forward of the driving wheels rather than behind them was Robert Stephenson's *Planet*. This engine, which had one pair of leading carrying wheels and one pair of driving wheels, was of 2–2–0 configuration whereas *Rocket* was an 0–2–2. It was delivered from the Stephenson works in Newcastle to the Liverpool & Manchester Railway only a month after the company had begun its service in September 1830.

Robert Stephenson achieved the objective of spreading the weight which necessarily went with increased power by using more axles. He did so with his *Patentee* of 1834, which was a 2–2–2 with one driving axle behind two carrying axles. Though the London & Birmingham continued to use 2–2–0s and 0–4–0s until 1845, *Patentee* was to establish a successful basis on which Stephenson and other builders could rely for future developments.

Meanwhile the Great Western Railway, with its 7ft 0¼in broad gauge, was setting a style and standard of construction which was soon to become widespread. Other railways had ordered locomotives from specialist builders almost 'off the shelf', choosing available types which seemed to suit their needs. Daniel Gooch, who had been appointed GWR Locomotive Superintendent in 1837 – just before his twenty-first birthday – was not impressed by the design or performance of some of the locomotives which had been ordered before his arrival. He eventually decided to lay down his own specifications. Among the engines which had been ordered prior to his appointment had been two from the Stephenson works at Newcastle where he had been employed. These 2–2–2s, *North Star* and *Morning Star*, had originally been ordered for the 5ft 6in gauge New Orleans Railway but the contract had been cancelled. They were converted to broad gauge for the GWR in 1837 and provided the young Gooch with his first reliable locomotives. Ten more, all bearing Star names, were bought by the company. Other generally similar 2–2–2s were ordered from different builders and later, engines of the 2–4–0 and 0–6–0 types were ordered for freight working. Some of the early 2–2–2s were converted to 4–2–2 tank engines and used on branch lines for many years.

The first of the engines built to Gooch's specifications to emerge from the GWR works at Swindon was the 2–2–2 *Great Western*, which was later to distinguish itself by running at an average speed of over 55mph on the round trip from Paddington to Exeter via Birstol and averaged 67mph between Paddington and Didcot during the gauge trials to which we have already referred. On a falling

This photograph of the preserved 0–4–2 *Lion* was taken during the filming of the *Titfield Thunderbolt* – a well-known Ealing Studios comedy of the mid-1950s. (P M Alexander)

gradient of 1-in-100 one 4–2–2 had already attained a speed of 78mph. *Great Western*'s average of 67mph was achieved when the locomotive was hauling a load of 60 tons over a distance of 53 miles. The performance was so spectacular that doubt was later cast on its feasibility. However, analysis of the known facts and technical data showed that a train of this power/weight ratio (around $4\frac{1}{2}$hp/ton) could have achieved such a performance. In 1848 GWR trains were regularly running the 53 miles from London to Didcot in between 48 and 50 minutes. *Great Western*, which came out in 1846, was followed by a few more 2–2–2s but then Gooch switched to a 4–2–2 configuration in 1847 with the Iron Dukes. Though by later standards these might appear to have been comparatively crude locomotives they proved eminently suited to travel at high speeds, hauling light loads along the superbly designed London-Bristol route engineered by Brunel. The Iron Dukes, of which 29 were built, had large boilers and fireboxes, 8ft diameter driving wheels and short piston strokes. With an all-up weight of 53 tons, they continued in production until 1855. By that time the pattern for the higher inter-city rail speeds of this century had been established, thanks to the combination of Gooch's engines and Brunel's broad gauge.

While the speed on the broad gauge was steadily increased, the smaller locomotives on the standard gauge could not match the GWR's performance, despite experiments with a number of designs intended to obtain greater power. There was a great fear that larger and higher boilers would induce engines to overturn if they were used on frames built for the narrower standard gauge. One attempt to lower the centre of gravity by matching a low-slung boiler with large driving wheels was made by Thomas Russell Crampton. He patented a locomotive on which the driving axle and big driving

An early experiment was Lane's 2–2–2 long boiler locomotive of 1849. Note the use of guard irons in front of the leading wheels, the continued use of 'concertina' type buffers and the haycock firebox. (The Science Museum)

42

wheels were located *behind* the boiler at the extreme rear, with only small carrying wheels beneath the boiler. Although Crampton's design achieved considerable success on the continent, it was not a high-speed locomotive and though stable it ran hard on the track. However it was a Crampton engine which probably came closest to broad-gauge standards of speed at that time when it ran the 41 miles from Wolverhampton to Coventry in 42 minutes.

Robert Stephenson also brought out a variation in design with his 4–2–0 'long boiler'. It was intended to increase thermal efficiency by making better use of the fuel through the increased heating surface of the longer tubes in the boiler, which also reduced the emission of hot cinders. For operating reasons the wheelbase had to be short. All the wheels were, therefore, placed in front of the firebox. As a result there was an overhang at the rear and this made the engine sway at speeds which would have resulted in considerable wear on the back wheels and could have caused accidents.

The largest wheel diameter ever employed on the standard gauge was the 8ft 6in of *Cornwall*, the famous engine built at Crewe in 1847 by Frances Trevithick, eldest son of Richard, for the LNWR. The boiler was slung below the driving axle, which passed through a channel formed in the top of the boiler. The rear carrying axle ran through the firebox in a transverse tube. In 1858, having put up no exceptional performances, *Cornwall* was rebuilt from a 4–2–2 to a conventional 2–2–2 with the boiler above the driving axle. It now performed better than its original configuration, though no better than other LNWR 2–2–2s with 7ft 6in diameter wheels. *Cornwall* is preserved in the National Railway Museum at York.

The designer for E B Wilson & Company of Leeds, David Joy, came out with a variation on the 2–2–2 which was to lead to future

The celebration to commemorate the centenary of the Liverpool & Manchester Railway in 1938 included the refurbishing and steaming of the *Lion* coupled to three first-class and three third-class replica coaches – a scenario repeated over 40 years later in the spring of 1980 during the RAIL 150 celebrations. (Cecil J Allen collection)

43

development. In 1846 he produced a 2–2–2 for the London, Brighton and South Coast Railway which had a fairly long wheelbase and 6ft diameter driving wheels set outside the frames and carrying wheels inside. This locomotive, named *Jenny Lind* after the contemporary Swedish soprano, had a boiler pressure of 120lb/sq in – unusually high for that period. The name was used for numerous successors and two of these went to the London & North Western Railway. Here they suggested to J E McConnell, the LNWR's Locomotive Superintendent, the idea of carrying *all* the wheels outside the frame. His first 2–2–2s from the company's Wolverton locomotive works came out in 1851 and, like the *Jenny Lind*s, had a long wheelbase. All the wheels were outside the frame. The exposed position of the 7ft drivers earned the engines the sobriquet 'Bloomers' (from the contemporary reformer of women's dress whose designs revealed that women had legs!). Further 'Bloomers' were produced with driving wheels of various diameters; they had a boiler pressure of 150lb/sq in and served the LNWR long and well in fast passenger traffic.

In response to a demand by the directors of the LNWR for the company to have locomotives capable of covering the journey from London to Birmingham in two hours, McConnell produced his Patent class of 2–2–2 in the early 1850s. These had 7ft 6in driving wheels and were criticized for their high centre of gravity. In fact their weaker feature proved to be the complicated boiler with a very large fire grate which McConnell intended to burn coal in place of the more expensive coke generally used. Eventually a brick arch and deflector plate were built into the firebox to provide an effective answer to the problem of size. The addition of the arch and downward-sloping deflector inside the firebox door ensured that air entering through the gate or firedoor remained in contact with the fire for as long as possible before reaching the boiler tubes. The arch was first used in 1850. Matthew Kirtley, Mechanical Engineer of the Midland Railway, later began experiments which proved the efficacy of the principle in 1859, after which time the arch and deflector plate became standard features of the steam locomotive's combustion system.

Like David Joy and McConnell, A Sturrock of the Great Northern also adopted high-boiler pressure. He built an experimental 4–2–2 which, though it had 7ft 6in driving wheels, strongly resembled Gooch's broad-gauge single-drivers. It had a boiler pressure of 150lb/sq in but did not put up any exceptional performances.

Another development which later became standard steam locomotion practice took place in the 1840s and involved the variable valve gear to control the distribution of steam to the cylinders. Devised at the Stephensons' works in 1841, it was called Stephenson's link motion. The refinement was an articulated linkage by means of which the travel of the valve could be varied and thus also the proportion of the piston stroke during which steam was admitted to the cylinders. For peak efficiency the admission period needed to be kept short so that steam already in the cylinder when the valve closed continued to work by expanding. In 1849 the Walschaerts valve gear linkage was introduced and remained in common use to the end of steam, its pattern of external rods and cranks easily recognised by enthusiasts.

Daniel Gooch, the Great Western Railways Chief Mechanical Engineer and later its Chairman, was responsible for these handsome 7ft 0¼in gauge 4–2–2 locomotives. (Colourviews Picture Library)

During the first 20 years or so of railways in Britain, development work was not confined to improving the locomotives or to finding stronger, more reliable materials for the track. The railway was a new concept relying on much new technology but it also made use initially of existing transport practices, adapting them as necessary. The builders of the first railway coaches, for example, had a ready-made prototype in the stage or mail carriages of the road. Road coaches usually had four seats inside and bench seats at the front and back of the roof, outside, which took a further ten people. Luggage was held on a rack on the roof while the mail and valuables were carried in a boot on the back.

The greater haulage capability of the steam locomotive meant that more people could be carried and the first railway coaches were built in the form of three or four road-style coaches mounted on a common frame. The broad gauge made it possible to seat eight passengers in a Great Western coach and even the standard gauge coaches were able to take six instead of four people in each section or compartment. Even so, the early carriages were only about six feet wide and they were for first-class passengers only. Some had a box seat for the guard and, like the road coaches, were fitted with rails round the roof so that luggage could be stowed there. To add extra brake power to that of the engine and tender, guards worked the handbrakes fitted to their own coaches.

From 1837 mail was carried by the railways and in 1838 the London & Birmingham Railway introduced a special coach for Post Office traffic with first-class passenger accommodation inside and the mail carried in boxes on the roof. Some coaches incorporated what looked like a projecting 'boot' at one end; rather than for stowing luggage, it was to enable a passenger lying on a paddle board across the seats to stretch his legs. The compartments were only five feet from side to side so that a passenger could not lie down unless there was this extra boot space. A coach of this type was used by the Dowager Queen Adelaide in 1842 and is now preserved in the National Railway Museum.

Second-class passengers who would have travelled on the roofs of road coaches – and could do so on a railway coach up to at least 1840 – were provided with the most basic of accommodation. Though the wagons were roofed they were usually open-sided so that even those passengers lucky enough to have a side wheel next to them still had

A model of a Bristol & Exeter Railway 7ft 0¼in gauge 4–2–2. The engine dates from 1849, was rebuilt in 1866 and became GWR No 2012. The model was made out of cardboard by E G Petrie in 1867. (Colourviews Picture Library)

to suffer the draughts. Third-class passengers were not catered for by some companies and by those who did carry them they were treated little better than animals, riding in open wagons which might, if they were lucky, have bench seats. Holes drilled in the floor prevented accumulations of water in wet weather but that was small comfort to passengers who were probably wet through anyway.

Legislation eventually improved the lot of all, but particularly the third-class passengers. A Select Committee of 1839 inquired into 'the state of communication by railway' and as a result the Regulation of Railway Acts of 1840 and 1842 established rules for the inspection of lines, safety in general and the fixing of fares. The Board of Trade in future included a Railway Department under an Inspector General of Railways. In 1844 Parliament insisted that third-class passengers must be catered for by all companies; the Regulations of Railways Act of that year laid down that at least one train in each direction every day on each line should provide third-class accommodation in closed carriages (roofed and glazed) with seats. The Act, which became known as the 'Cheap Trains Act', also stipulated that trains were to pick up and set down at every station and that their speed must be at least 12mph. The fare was not to exceed one penny per mile. To mark their objection some companies ran the trains at inconvenient times.

By this time second-class coaches had glazed windows and some padding on seats. First-class compartments had plush interiors, padded cushions, partitions and curtains. The third-class accommodation for the 'Parliamentary trains' marked a considerable

Furness Railway's 2–4–0 No 2 of class E1. These engines were built by Sharp Stewart & Company in 1870 and subsequently rebuilt as shown here in 1896. (P B Whitehouse collection)

improvement: coaches were usually four-wheelers, often very well protected from the weather because there were few windows, had wooden bench seats but otherwise bare interiors without partitions.

As traffic increased it became necessary to control the movement of trains. Fortunately, electrical science was developing at the same time as the railways. Though the electric telegraph was demonstrated between Euston Station and Camden in 1838 it was not widely used for some years, either because staff were not literate enough to use it or because companies could see no financial advantage. Later its principles were widely used to provide signalmen with a means of communicating details of train movements. Signalling was rudimentary initially, generally relying on men described as 'policemen' to give hand signals to drivers indicating whether they must stop, slow down or proceed at full speed. The railway police were also responsible for the security of lines and stations.

Mechanical signalling methods gradually took over from hands and flags. They were usually worked by policemen stationed at individual signals. One of the earliest and most recognisable as the forefather of the railway signal (used universally before coloured lights became common) was introduced on the Liverpool & Manchester Railway in 1834. It was a red-painted swivelling board which was turned to face the driver of an oncoming train if it had to stop, and aligned edge-on if the line was clear. Edge-on the board was barely visible from a distance, thereby complying with the early principle that absence of a signal indicated a clear track. In time, however, it was realised that a definite 'clear-track' signal was desir-

47

able and in 1838 the GWR introduced a swivelling signal with a disc and a crossbar mounted at right angles to each other. Positive danger was indicated by the bar being face on, clear by the disc face on. Since there was still no communication between stations the 'clear' indication was no absolute guarantee of an open line ahead.

With individually controlled signals a train was, at first, allowed to proceed if the policeman judged that sufficient time had elapsed since the last train had gone ahead. In some cases policemen were instructed to stop fast trains and tell the driver how long it had been since the last train had passed. This put the onus on the driver to regulate his speed. Such an imprecise system could be dispensed with when the electric telegraph was introduced. A signalman – the policemen's duties were soon split between men specialising in particular jobs – could ask his colleague along the line whether the previous train had reached or passed the next signalling point and whether the next train could proceed. The line was divided into sections with a signalman at both ends and only one train was allowed on each section at a time. The 'block section' system, as it was called, came into use on some lines in the early 1840s.

The next step from a signalman patrolling the signals and points under his control to operate them individually was to bring the means of operation together in his shelter. The shelter developed into the signalbox and as more levers working signals and points came under the control of one man, methods were devised to guard against conflicting signals being displayed. It was, for example, essential to ensure that if points and signals had been set to clear one route, the levers controlling signals and points on a converging route were locked to danger. Such equipment was first seen in primitive form in the 1840s. In the same decade came the semaphore signal, with an arm held horizontally for danger and inclined down 45 degrees for caution and vertically down for clear.

As main lines were built throughout the country, stations were erected to serve towns and villages along the routes, or even merely close to them. Many country stations had sidings for goods traffic so that freight could be sent to places that, before the railway came, could only be reached by horse-drawn wagon. By the middle of the nineteenth century railways were becoming established as part of everyday life. Long journeys could now be measured in terms of hours rather than days and goods had a countrywide distribution network. In just a few years a way of life that had lasted for centuries had been changed forever.

A 1979-built replica of George Stephenson's famous steam locomotive *Rocket* on show in Hyde Park, London, during August of that year. (C M Whitehouse)

An LNWR official postcard of 1904 compares freight trains of 1837 with LNWR's then-modern compound 0–8–0 at work hauling a heavy train over Shap Fell. (P B Whitehouse collection)

Kept to run one of the Director's
saloons on the LNWR, this strange
single wheeler survives today in the
National Collection. No 3020
Cornwall is shown here 'at home'
in Crewe Works. (John Adams)

The London & North Western
Railway 2–4–0 No 790 *Hardwicke* is
now preserved in the National
Railway Museum, York. This
famous engine participated in the
'Race to the North' in 1895.
(C M Whitehouse)

right:
The Highland Railway around the turn of the century. This painting by J D Goffey shows one of the celebrated *Skye Bogie* 4–4–0s No 85 at Kyle of Lochalsh. (Colourviews Picture Library)

far right:
Midland Railway single wheeler No 118 (now preserved) shows clearly the fine standard of painting with the earlier diamond shaped coat of arms on the splasher. (John Adams)

left:
This Highland Railway Jones Goods
class 4–6–0 No 103 is now preserved.
This engine was returned to service
for a few years in the early 1960s
for special enthusiast excursions.
(P B Whitehouse)

below:
Oban station in Edwardian days
(from a painting by F Moore) shows
the magnificent livery of the
Caledonian Railway's locomotives.
(Colourviews Picture Library)

below:
Virtually all the pre-Grouping railways carried their own crests or coats of arms either on the locomotive and/or coaches. This example was used by the South Eastern & Chatham Railway. (Colourviews Picture Library)

right:
London Brighton and South Coast Railway's 4–4–0 No 64 *Norfolk* heads a Brighton express in the 1911 livery of amber brown. From a painting by F Moore. (Colourviews Picture Library)

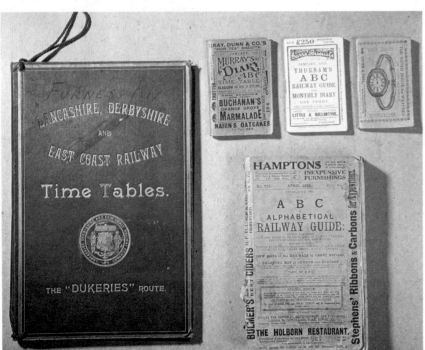

left:
A rare example of the Lancashire, Derbyshire & East Coast Railway timetable plus examples of the many ABC types of table available throughout the country. (P B Whitehouse collection)

far left:
This notice advertising the Great Northern Railway Company's hotels would have been affixed to a panel above the seats in first- and second-class coaches to ensure that passengers were fully aware of the services offered. Most of the larger railway companies owned and ran their own hotels. (Colourviews Picture Library)

top left:
A North Eastern Railway class Atlantic No 726 takes an express to the north out of York. From a painting by F Moore. (Colourviews Picture Library)

middle left:
Drummonds T14 class 4–6–0 'Paddle Box', designed for the London & South Western Railway in 1911, was so nicknamed because of its large splashers. No 443 of the

class is shown in this painting by
C Hamilton Ellis heading a
Bournemouth-London (Waterloo)
express passing Beaulieu Road in
1913. (Viscount Garnock collection)

bottom left:
Robert H Whitelegg's massive
4–6–4T of the Glasgow & South
Western Railway heads a Stranraer-
to-Glasgow (St Enoch) boat express
near Ibrox in 1922. By D Goffey.
(Colourviews Picture Library)

above:
H A Ivatt's Great Northern Railway
4–4–2 Atlantic No 280 leaves the
south entrance of Hadley Wood
tunnel with an up express during
Edwardian days. From a painting by
F Moore. (E S Russell collection)

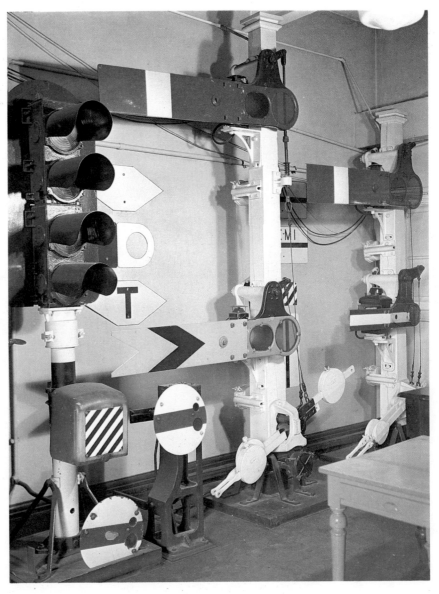

above:
Example of signals as presented at the British Rail signalling school. On the left, multi-aspect colour lights; below, ground or shunting signals; centre, upper quadrant home and distant arms; and right, upper quadrant shunting and *calling on* signal arms. (Colourviews Picture Library)

left:
An LNER manually operated signal box on the East Coast main line. Note the coloured levers, red for stop signals, yellow for distant signals and black for points. From the original painting by Terence Cuneo. (Courtesy British Railways)

above:
End of an era: Few London & North
Western Railway passenger engines
survived the Stanier and beyond the
1930s but World War II prolonged an
odd lifespan. Here is one of the
Prince of Wales class 4–6–0s to escape
the torch until just after the war –
No 25673 *Lusitania* at New Street
station Birmingham.
(P B Whitehouse)

left:
Island Railway: The last remaining
steam section on the Isle of Wight
was the line from Ryde to Ventnor.
Since early Southern days most
passenger trains were worked by these
Adams 0–4–4 tanks built for the
London & South Western Railway.
This scene shows a train entering
Ventnor in 1960.
(P M Alexander)

5
RAILWAYS SUPREME

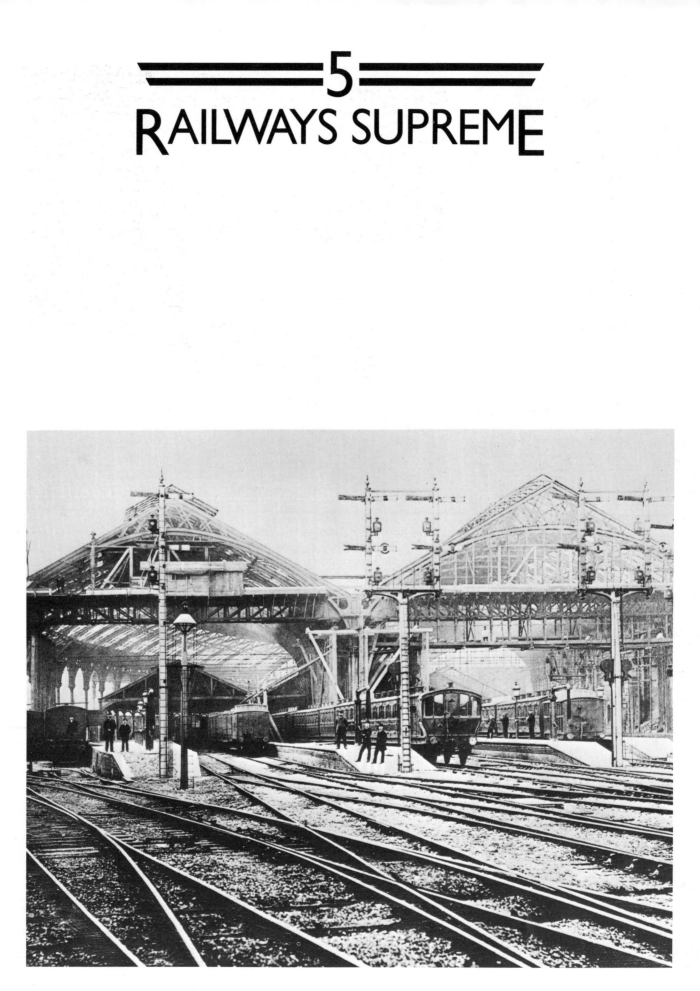

The second half of the nineteenth century was marked by the virtual completion of the British railway map with infilling by more main lines, cross-country routes and branch lines. There were also the development of railway empires, ruthless competition between companies providing rival services over similar routes, and the emergence of strong-willed personalities who led those companies.

The London & North Western Railway rose to a dominant position by further acquisitions after its formation from the amalgamation of the London & Birmingham, the Grand Junction and the Manchester & Birmingham railways. It encouraged and supported acquisitions by other companies if these were thought to be to the LNWR's advantage, and prompted nominally independent companies to keep intruders out of North Western territory. It pressed the Chester & Holyhead Railway to speed up its construction work so that the LNWR could secure the Irish Mail traffic and prevent the GWR from winning the traffic for its own service via Fishguard. The Chester & Holyhead was taken over by the LNWR in 1858.

Euston was regarded by the LNWR as the 'Gateway to the North' and the Great Northern's projected line to London was seen as a threat of serious competition for traffic between London and the North of England. Already in existence was the LNWR's own route from Euston to the Midlands, Yorkshire and the North East by way of Rugby. However, despite LNWR opposition, the Great Northern reached its first London terminus at Maiden Lane in 1850.

Led by its General Manager, Captain Mark Huish, the LNWR also obstructed the Great Western Railway in its bid to extend north-westwards from Banbury to Birmingham, Chester and Merseyside. The Shrewsbury & Chester and Shrewsbury & Birmingham companies fought against the obstruction in alliance with the GWR but the other line involved, that from Birkenhead to Chester, had already become a satellite of the LNWR and in 1850 it was persuaded by devious and underhand means to handle Shrewsbury & Chester traffic. The GWR and the Shrewsbury companies re-

right:
Brunel's 7ft 0¼in gauge for the Great Western Railway ensured steady running at high speeds for the day. Logic ensured that it could not survive as the remainder of Britain's Railway system evolved around the standard, or 4ft 8½in gauge. Here is Bridgend station in South Wales in the later days of the 7ft 0¼in gauge, 1878. (National Railway Museum)

left:
Brighton terminus 1862 – note the ornate station roof, the slotted post signals and the 'birdcage' roof (for the guard's lookout) on the four-wheeled coaches centre left and right. (National Railway Museum)

sponded by obtaining running powers over the Birkenhead line by Act of Parliament in 1851. When, encouraged by the LNWR, the Birkenhead company sought to withdraw from the agreement, Parliament intervened again. At last it was clear that the powerful LNWR alliance could be challenged successfully.

The meandering route of the GWR (the 'Great Way Round', according to cynics) to Exeter via Bristol left a big area further south open to railway development. The London & South Western Railway had extended in 1847 from Bishopstoke (Eastleigh) to Salisbury, which was later to be on its main line to the West Country. In the late 1840s, however, the company planned to serve Exeter via Dorchester and opened the Southampton & Dorchester Railway the same year as the Salisbury branch. The Southampton & Dorchester was planned as a broad-gauge line by local businessmen who had originally intended to lease it to the GWR. However, as the result of a deal between the GWR and LSWR, it went to the latter. In return the LSWR agreed to leave railway development in west Cornwall to the GWR. The London & South Western extended its service to Weymouth from Dorchester in 1857 by obtaining running powers over GWR tracks, while GWR trains continued to serve Dorchester via Swindon and Westbury.

The Great Western Railway's tunnel under the river Severn greatly reduced the distance and therefore the train times to South Wales. Construction of this masterpiece in civil engineering began in 1875 and the work was completed in 1886. (National Railway Museum)

First ticket issued by the Great Western Railway, Bristol to Cardiff via the Severn Tunnel, 1 December 1886. (P B Whitehouse collection)

Last days of Brunel's dream – scene at Teignmouth, south Devon, shows the down 'Cornishman' in May 1892, just prior to final gauge conversion. Note the short sleepers already cut and laid nearby. The locomotive is a small 'convertible' 2-4-0. (C J Allen collection)

The West of England main line from Reading to Exeter via Newbury and Westbury, with a junction for Yeovil and Dorchester at Castle Cary, was formed from a number of minor lines and was not completed until 1906. The route to Exeter opened by the LSWR in July 1860 was from a junction with the Southampton line west of Basingstoke, through Salisbury and Honiton. Overcoming numerous objections and obstructions the LSWR went beyond Exeter north of Dartmoor and down to Plymouth. It opened a through service from London Waterloo to that city in 1876 and completed its penetration of the area with the opening of its line to Padstow on 27 March 1899.

The GWR and LSWR covered individual areas west of Plymouth but for traffic between Plymouth and Exeter and on to London, particularly for Atlantic liners calling at Plymouth, the two companies ran fast overnight trains. Both also developed important holiday traffic, the GWR to resorts west of Exeter and the LSWR to north Cornwall and places on the south Devon coast east of Exeter which were not served by the GWR.

South of London the LSWR competed with the London, Brighton and South Coast Railway for Portsmouth and Isle of Wight traffic. When the first LSWR trains tried to get through in January 1859

Victorian country station: Market Bosworth station (Leicestershire) in 1883 with Midland Railway single-wheeler 2–2–2 No 35 (shedded at Coalville) in the platform. Note the typical small goods yard for local trade and traffic including a cattle dock, coal yard and covered goods shed. (R E Tustin collection)

there were fights at Havant. The LBSCR also competed with the South Eastern Railway for traffic on routes along the Kent and Sussex borders.

Sir Edward Watkin, Chairman of the South Eastern at the time, had earlier played a large part in the sale of the Trent Valley Railway in Staffordshire, of which he was Secretary, to the LNWR, the board of which he also joined. In 1853 Watkin became General Manager of the Manchester, Sheffield & Lincolnshire Railway. There he gradually loosened the company's ties with the LNWR and worked up a closer relationship with the Great Northern. He became Chairman of the MS & LR in 1864 and worked vigorously to fulfil his ambition to bring the Sheffield-based company to London. That, however, took nearly 30 years and a long Parliamentary struggle before a Bill for the London extension received the Royal assent in 1893. Meanwhile, Watkin had become Chairman of the South Eastern Railway in 1866 and of the Metropolitan Railway in 1872. He also took an interest in the newly formed Channel Tunnel company. Collectively these wide interests made possible the eventual through-running of trains between Manchester and the Channel ports, via the Metropolitan, the East London and the South Eastern railways, and – given a Channel tunnel – on to the Continent. However, the grand dream of a Manchester-Paris express was not to become reality. Watkin resigned all his chairmanships because of

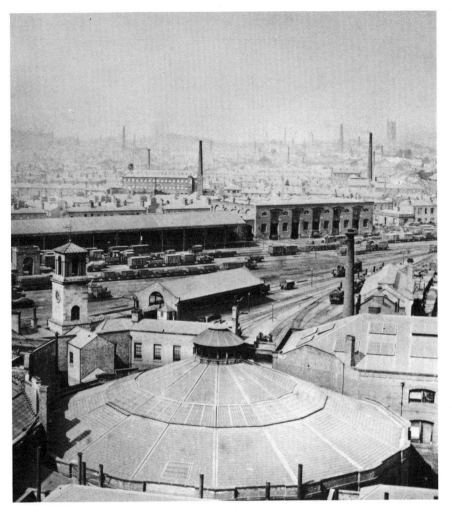

Derby from the Midland Railway roundhouse in 1860. (National Railway Museum)

A portrait of a guard in full dress on the Cambrian Railways. (Colourviews Picture Library)

ill health only a year after the Manchester, Sheffield & Lincolnshire Railway's extension to London received approval. Watkin's withdrawal brought to an end much of the inter-company squabbling which, while it achieved some worthwhile results, had delayed some important developments.

Even so, while these battles had been going on, extensions of railway service were carried out elsewhere in the British Isles. Cambrian Railways, for example, had a main line crossing Wales from Welshpool to Barmouth and Aberystwyth, and a branch southwards from Moat Lane Junction to Brecon, where it joined the Brecon & Methyr line from over the border. The North Wales coast was served by the LNWR while South and West Wales were GWR territory. There were also various small companies linking the coal mines of the South Wales valleys with the steelworks and ports. As Welsh industry expanded the LNWR made further inroads, serving isolated areas in South Wales reached by jointly worked lines and also obtaining running powers to major centres, even to Swansea, Llandrindod Wells and Llanwrtyd Wells.

The early advance of railways in East Anglia was a slow process, dogged by low traffic and a shortage of capital. Moreover, the first company to turn its attentions north-eastwards from London, the Eastern Counties Railway, caused itself added problems by adopting a track gauge of 5ft. It took some years to realise the error of its

Bletchley station *circa* 1900. A Webb Compound 2–2–2 No 644 *Vesuvius* double-heads a Precedent class 2–4–0 on a long Cambridge train. Unfortunately the identity of neither engine is known. (Colourviews Picture Library)

ways and convert to standard gauge. By the time the ECR reached Colchester in 1843, another company, the Eastern Union, had stepped in and completed a line to Norwich. The ECR was naturally furious and for five years it persistently created difficulties at Colchester, where the two companies' trains connected. In 1854 it took over the EUR. Meanwhile, in 1845, the ECR also reached Norwich over an easier route via Cambridge and Ely. In 1846 it proposed a branch from Ely to Peterborough, intending to establish its own London–York route, but Parliament decided that the Great Northern Railway's scheme should go ahead instead.

The Great Eastern Railway's London terminus, Liverpool Street, which opened in stages between 1874 and 1875, eventually became another starting point for the north as well as for East Anglia. The Great Eastern was created in 1862 by mergers of the East Anglian companies and their various offshoots which ran inland and to coastal towns such as Harwich and Yarmouth. Between 1879 and 1882 the Great Eastern agreed to operate jointly with the Great Northern on a cross-country route from March, near Ely, to Doncaster via Spalding, Sleaford, Lincoln and Gainsborough. When the North Eastern granted the GER running powers north of Doncaster, the Great Eastern was able to establish a through express passenger service from Liverpool Street to York.

In 1876 a third Anglo-Scottish main line was opened, extending the influence of the Midland Railway from South Wales to the Clyde Valley. Despite earlier quarrels the Great Northern allowed the Midland access to Kings Cross via a GNR line from Leicester to Hitchin which had opened in 1857, but the GNR would not allow Midland Railway trains to use the track from Hitchin into Kings Cross at the expense of its own services. The Midland endured the

An LNWR 'Lady of the Lake' class 2–2–2 with a 15-coach train made up of eight-wheeled bogie and six-wheeled stock (about 1900) heads up the West Coast main line. The second and third vehicles carry destination boards. (Colourviews Picture Library)

top right:
Great Eastern Railway up express on Ipswich troughs with rebuilt T19 2–4–0 No 1022 later rebuilt as a 4–4–0 in 1900. (Colourviews Picture Library)

difficulties thus created until 1863, when it gained Parliamentary approval to build a new line from Bedford via St Albans into St Pancras terminus, opened in 1868.

The next Midland Railway goal was Manchester, which presented the challenge of beating the LNWR for London business. In 1867 the Midland opened an extension to Manchester of its Amber-gate-Buxton branch. This involved boring the $1\frac{3}{4}$-mile Dove Holes tunnel through the Peak Forest hills.

The LNWR retaliated against the Midland's invasion of London by extending its influence in Cumbria. Here the Midland's traffic for Carlisle over the Clapham-Ingleton branch of the Settle/Lancaster/Morecambe line had to use the LNWR's main line over Shap. The Midland did not want to build its own route over those fells, which would have been an extremely expensive operation. The LNWR deliberately prolonged difficulties over joint operation between Ingleton and Carlisle and in 1866 the Midland embarked on its own Settle & Carlisle line. This is without doubt the wildest and grandest trunk route in Britain, with long, tough gradients, 19 viaducts and more than three miles of tunnels. After completing this line in 1876 the Midland opened its through service from London to Scotland, operating in conjunction with the Glasgow & South Western to Glasgow, and the North British to Edinburgh.

In the west of Scotland generally the Caledonian and Glasgow & South Western systems intertwined. In some areas they worked harmoniously together but in others less peacefully, particularly on the Clyde coast, where they competed fiercely for traffic. The Caledonian operated the Glasgow, Narrhead and Kilmarnock line jointly with the G&SWR, although the route helped the rival Anglo-Scottish service. A similar partnership covered the exit from Glasgow to Paisley. The two companies also shared a Glasgow terminus at Bridge Street until 1879, when the G&SWR opened St Enoch station and the Caledonian moved to Glasgow Central.

In eastern Scotland the completion of the Forth Bridge in 1890 established the North British Railway as another trunk system. The bridge was made accessible to both Edinburgh and Glasgow traffic by means of a triangular junction built into the inter-city line. North of the river a more direct route from Edinburgh to Perth was opened in 1883 and Kinnaber Junction and Aberdeen were reached with the grant of running powers over the Caledonian's tracks approaching that city.

For about 20 years, from the mid-1840s, Aberdeen had been regarded as the future gateway for railways penetrating the Highlands. In fact the route built north of Perth across the Grampian mountains to Inverness via Forres in 1863 became the Highland Railway in 1865. A line was extended further northwards to Dingwall and Skye in 1870 and the main route opened to Wick and Thurso in 1874. The Skye line was extended to Kyle of Lochalsh in 1897 and in 1898 the Highland Railway opened the direct route from Aviemore to Inverness. Between Aviemore and Blair Atholl the British Rail system reaches its highest main line point at 1484ft on the summit at Druimuachdar.

The Scottish railway system was rounded off by the acquisition in 1870 by the Caledonian of a company which was building north-westward from Callander. Eventually the line twisted and climbed its way to Oban by way of the Pass of Brander after the Caledonian completed construction work, and when the route was opened in July 1880 it attracted considerable tourist traffic. Finally the spectacular West Highland line to Fort William was opened in August 1894, and was extended to Mallaig in 1901.

Railway expansion in the United Kingdom had virtually ceased

Vital bridge: The building of the Forth and Tay bridges considerably shortened the East Coast partners route to Aberdeen. The grandeur of the great cantilevers of the Forth Bridge still appeals today when the smokestains have been weathered away from the approach arches. (Colourviews Picture Library)

The first two return tickets, London to Manchester and back, were issued at the then-new Marylebone station, 15 March 1899. (Colourviews Picture Library)

below:
The final trunk route to be built (and the first to go) was the Manchester, Sheffield & Lincoln's extension south to London (Marylebone via Leicester and Rugby). This picture shows an inaugural train running into Brackley station on the opening day, 9 March 1899. From then on the railway was named the Great Central. (Leicester Library)

by the beginning of the twentieth century and it was becoming evident that despite Parliamentary controls many areas of the country were already over-endowed with railways. The resulting multiplicity of separately owned stations, depots, yards and competing lines proved a major economic disadvantage, the effects of which have endured to the present day.

Passenger comfort in the closing decade of the Victorian era was one of extreme contrasts. It could still be an austere, trying and wearisome business or a matter of comparative luxury. Passengers were wise to set out with greatcoats and rugs and flasks. They were drawn along in bone-shaking four- or six-wheel carriages which were lit by smelly oil lamps but had no heating. There were no corridors and usually no toilet facilities. Usually journeys were not more than seven or eight hours long – except on Anglo-Scottish runs and those from London to the extreme South West – and these conditions seemed to have been mutely endured. However, an approach to better standards had begun in the 1870s when the Pullman Palace Car Company's superior coaches were introduced in Britain.

George Mortimer Pullman had formed the company in the United States in 1867 to build the higher grade of accommodation required for long-distance trains undertaking journeys of several days. In 1872 the General Manager of the Midland Railway, James Allport, visited the United States and recognised that the Pullmans might be a way of achieving the company's objective of offering better accommodation than its rivals. The Midland had that year taken the contentious step of providing third-class facilities on all its trains. Now a contract was drawn up for 18 Pullman cars to be shipped in parts to England and assembled at the Derby works. Day and night Pullman services were inaugurated between St Pancras and Bradford in 1874. The complete Pullman trains included second-

Midland and Great Northern
Railway 4–4–0 No 55 with a train
of six-wheeled stock in 1901.
(Colourviews Picture Library)

class and third-class accommodation as well as parlour and sleeping cars for first-class passengers. Two years later the Midland's Anglo-Scottish express service included first-class Pullman drawing-room cars for day trains and sleepers on night runs. The Midland had made the astute move of re-classifying second-class travel as third-class and using second-class carriages as thirds. Thereafter all third-class passenger rolling stock was built to what had previously been second-class standards, with padded seats and backs. At a time when other companies were still using rigid wheelbase six-wheeler coaches on expresses, Midland passengers on the Anglo-Scottish service rode in comfort in compartment coaches carried on bogies.

Strangely, it was these compartment coaches which, in the long term proved more popular than the first-class Pullmans with their armchair seating, lamp-lit tables, toilet facilities and centre gangway layout. Even so, the credit for a change of heart by other companies in their design of passenger accommodation must go to the Midland for its introduction of Pullmans and the standard of its own coach-building. Pullman cars were used by a few other com-

top right:
The cover of the working timetable issued by the London Brighton & South Coast Railway in conjunction with the special train for the Shah of Persia, 5 July 1873. (P B Whitehouse collection)

right:
Alresford station (now on a section of preserved railway) Southern Region British Railways in 1951. This station, once on the Alton to Winchester branch of the London & South Western railway, depicts an example of a one-time numerous but now almost extinct amenity. (Colourviews Picture Library)

panies, including sleepers on the East Coast route and day-time parlour cars on the London–Brighton service. They lasted longest on the short south coast journeys.

The first sleeping cars had been introduced in Britain shortly before Pullmans were imported; the Ashbury Railway Carriage and Iron Company built a six-wheel convertible for use on the East Coast route in 1873 and in the same year the LNWR introduced a sleeping car of its own design on the Euston–Glasgow service. The Pullman retained, for a time, the advantage of having its own built-in hot water heating system. The normal method of heating in lesser passenger coaches was the footwarmer, a type of hot water bottle which passengers hired at various stations. The low-pressure steam method of heating passenger rolling stock was not introduced until 1884 and it was another 20 years before nearly all trains were fitted.

In 1879 a kitchen was built into a Pullman car on the Great Northern. It was demonstrated on a run from London to Peterborough and then used regularly from November of that year for first-class passengers on the Leeds–Kings Cross service. It was the first regular railway dining car with meals cooked on board in Britain. Passengers using the service paid the full Pullman supplement. Although some coaches at this time had corridors there was still no communication between coaches and this restricted the use of a restaurant service. In 1891 the Great Eastern introduced a set of four six-wheeled coaches which had inter-connections. One coach of the set, which

One of Patrick Stirling's 4–2–2 express engines, built for the Great Northern Railway, was used in the famous 'Race to the North' against the West Coast companies. Relegated to more menial tasks in 1901, No 1004 is still spotlessly clean. (Colourviews Picture Library)

was used on the 'North Country Continental' from Harwich, was a first-class dining car while the third-class passengers, who were not admitted to this car, had a folding table on which meals were served from the kitchen in one coach only. It was the GWR which introduced the first non-Pullman corridor train with vestibule connections between the coaches on the London–Birkenhead service in 1892. It did not have restaurant facilities. From 1893 East and West Coast companies introduced complete corridor restaurant-car trains available to all classes.

Despite some tentative experiments with gas lighting, oil lamps predominated into the early 1890s. Lighting by gas produced from oil was tested in an LNWR express in 1875 and first installed widely by the Metropolitan Railway in London in 1876. Experiments with electric lighting were carried out by the London, Brighton & South Coast Railway in 1881, using batteries in a single Pullman and then, in 1889, a dynamo on a four-car Pullman train. The dynamo was belt-driven from the axles and charged the batteries, thus being the forerunner of the standard system employing a dynamo under every coach.

Though the steam train was the fastest means of transport in Victorian years, it was still not as fast as it could have been. Speeds were generally set below those which locomotives were capable of achieving because of the lack of sufficiently powerful brakes, problems of signal spacing, traffic density and the curvature of track – all of

Towards the end of the nineteenth century F W Webb, the Chief Mechanical Engineer to the London & North Western Railway, built several experimental series of compound locomotives using two high- and one low-pressure cylinders. The earlier 2–2–2–0s did not have coupled wheels! These somewhat unsuccessful engines were comparatively short-lived though during their heyday they worked the principle express trains. Shown here is No 519 *Shooting Star* at Chester with a local train around 1900, after being put out to grass by Webb's successor George Whale. (P B Whitehouse collection)

Caledonian Railway 4–4–0 No 729 (later LMS No 14319) of McIntosh Dunalastair I class. (Cecil J Allen collection)

One of William Stroudley's
Gladstone class 0–4–2 locomotives
No 188 *Allen Sarle*. These London
Brighton & South Coast Railway
engines were kept so clean that it was
said that a finger would be unmarked
if wiped on the paintwork. The
scene is Oxted, Surrey in 1901.
(Colourviews Picture Library)

Ex-Highland Railway *Small Ben*
class 4–4–0 in early LMS livery (coat
of arms on cab side and number on
tender – Midland fashion) stands on
the turntable to Thurso in May 1928.
(H C Casserley)

below:
A Midland Railways express train
makes a water stop at Bedford
behind Johnson 4–2–2 No 176 about
1900. (Colourviews Picture Library)

which had to be considered in planning timetables. There were two famous occasions when locomotives were pushed to their limits on the East and West Coast routes. These were in the so-called 'Railway Races' from London to Edinburgh in 1888 and to Aberdeen in 1895.

The announcement by the Great Northern in 1887 that it would admit third-class passengers to its daily morning expresses between London and Scotland which at that time took nine hours to reach Edinburgh was the spur which brought about the first of the races. The West Coast expresses from Euston already took third-class passengers but the journey took ten hours. Accordingly the partners involved in this route replied in the summer of 1888 with the announcement that from 2 June the morning express from Euston would also cover the Edinburgh run in nine hours. A series of leap-frogging moves continued throughout that summer until 13 August, when the East Coast companies scheduled their Kings Cross express to reach Edinburgh in just 7 hours 45 minutes. The first train on this new schedule was late but on the same day the Euston train reached Edinburgh in 7 hours 38 minutes. The East Coast made the run in 7 hours 32 minutes the next day. Such timings were, in fact, impractical for regular operation and thereafter by mutual consent the East Coast set a time of 8 hours 15 minutes and the West Coast 8 hours 30 minutes, the latter's route being 7¾ miles longer.

When the Forth Bridge was opened in 1890 it made the route between Kings Cross to Aberdeen 16 miles shorter than that from Euston. The East Coast companies set out to exploit this advantage when the Highlands began to attract an increasing tourist traffic. Thus in the summer of 1895 another 'race' was joined between the two rival partnerships. The two overnight express routes converged at Kinnaber Junction, 38 miles south of Aberdeen and from there the East Coast train ran over the line of the Caledonian, a member of the

Three of these ancient London & South Western Railway Beattie 2–4–0 tanks were kept specially for service over the Wenford bridge mineral branch in Cornwall. Here is the daily goods train at Helland behind No 30585 as late as September 1959. (Derek Cross)

West Coast partnership. On one occasion, when the contest was at its height, the signalman at Kinnaber Junction, who was employed by the Caledonian, was offered both the expresses at the same time. Sportingly, he gave the road to the East Coast rival, which reached Aberdeen from Kings Cross in 8 hours 40 minutes – two minutes longer than the best East Coast time, achieved on 22 August. On that day the West Coast train completed its run in 8 hours 32 minutes for an overall average speed of more than 60mph, despite stops at Crewe, Carlisle, Stirling and Perth. The highest start-to-stop average speed of 67.2mph was achieved on the Preston to Carlisle section, over Shap, by the 2–4–0 *Hardwicke*.

Although train weights were reduced to uneconomic levels for these special efforts, the performances achieved were remarkable for the time. By the end of the first 50 years of Britain's railways the average train speed for passenger expresses was just over 40mph, allowing for intermediate stops. That average was substantially above performances elsewhere and even in countries such as the United States and in Europe it was not equalled until after the turn of the century.

The key to higher speed was better braking. Early locomotive designers were unwilling to fit brakes directly to engines and even as late as the 1870s many passenger trains ran with brakes on tenders and brake vans at the front and back of the train. Guards worked the brakes by hand, obeying whistle signals from the drivers.

After witnessing an appalling train crash, the American George Westinghouse started work to improve braking and he patented the continuous compressed-air brake system in 1873. Its essential features were that the brakes could be applied throughout the train by the driver and that if the train parted while on the move the brakes on both sections were automatically applied. Though the system was eventually adopted by some British companies, most chose instead the continuous vacuum brake – a simpler and cheaper but less powerful and slower-acting alternative. This later proved a major technical handicap in the modernisation of stock by British Railways.

William Stroudley designed these almost evergreen little tank engines for use on the London Brighton & South Coast Railway in Victorian days. So useful were they that some, when redundant, were sold out of service to smaller and minor lines; others lasted well into British Railway's ownership.
Southern Railway No W3 *Carisbrooke* was sold by the LBSCR to the Isle of Wight Railway and taken over at Grouping thus rejoining the fold. (H C Casserley)

Back in the 1870s and 1880s most companies were reluctant to adopt continuous braking because it involved the expensive business of fitting brakes to all vehicles. When they did adopt the system it was generally fitted only to passenger vehicles. However, after a catastrophe at Armagh in 1889 when 78 people were killed in an accident which could have been prevented by continuous braking and the block section signal system with the electric telegraph, Parliament made the installation of both mandatory.

The end of the broad gauge on the GWR had become accepted by the 1870s and some of the company's goods tank engines built in 1872 were constructed so that they could be converted to standard gauge. In addition broad gauge locomotive design was allowed to stagnate for more than 30 years, up to the GWR's eventual conversion to standard gauge in 1892. In the meantime the standard-gauge railways were producing locomotives capable of matching the performance of those of the GWR.

During the 1870s the majority of British express passenger engines were of 2–2–2, 4–2–2, 2–4–0 or 4–4–0 configurations. With the standard of track greatly improved so that the steel lines were strong and firm, the six-wheeled engines were performing safely and well at high speeds. There were some notable performers among the 2–4–0s, of which the Kirtley 800 class of the Midland and the 901 class of the North Eastern were outstanding. But the first standard-gauge engines really to rival the GWR's broad-gauge types were the Stirling 4–2–2s. These had 8ft diameter driving wheels and outside cylinders and were built for the Great Northern from 1870 onwards. The famous Stirling single No 1 is preserved as part of the national railway collection. Earlier Stirling engines were six-wheelers with inside cylinders; Stirling made the change to lower the boiler and improve stability and incidentally produced a locomotive with considerably more graceful lines than most contemporaries. The stability of the Stirling design was underlined in the slightly later 2–2–2s with 7ft 6in driving wheels and inside cylinders. The two types were used on similar duties with little difference in performance. The Stirling singles continued to be built until 1893–94 and it was amply proved that, in favourable conditions, engines with single driving axles performed well. Less power was absorbed in the drive than was the case in coupled engines of the same size, so more was available at the drawbar. However, under conditions that made the driving wheels slip, such as a sudden rainstorm, the pulling power of the engine was frequently reduced. Many companies came to consider the 2–4–0 and 4–4–0 as more suitable for everyday work, despite the improvement in tractive ability brought about by the Holt sand blast in the mid-1880s. This used steam or compressed air to blow sand under the driving wheels to provide a better grip on the rails.

The Midland had a very similar experience to the Great Northern with its Johnson inside-cylinder 4–2–2s with drivers of up to 7ft 4in. The first of several batches of these appeared in 1884. Alongside similarly powered Johnson 4–4–0s, the difference in performance was not significant; the singles were occasionally outstanding and it was generally thought that they were lighter on coal but the coupled engines were more reliable in bad weather. Several classes of Webb

A Stirling 4–4–0 heads a train of six wheelers somewhere in the London area around the turn of the century. Note the safety valves on top of the dome, the Westinghouse brake pump ahead of the leading driving wheel splasher and the outside springing of the small tender. (C J Allen collection)

George Jackson Churchward's four-cylinder 4–6–0 Star class when new in 1910. Note the 3500-gallon tender. The coaches were then in red/brown livery. The locomotive is No 4035 *Queen Charlotte*. (Cecil J Allen collection)

engines on the LNWR were intended to combine the good qualities of single and coupled drive by having two separate (that is, uncoupled) driving axles driven by separate cylinders. On simple-expansion four cylinder engines the results were indifferent but on three-cylinder compound classes, good performance and fuel economy were achieved, though not necessarily only – or even mainly – because of the uncoupled four-wheel drive.

Performance capability of Caledonian Railway passenger locomotives was advanced considerably in 1896 with the introduction of the McIntosh Dunalastair class, which was little more than a standard 4–4–0 design fitted with a bigger boiler. The favourable results with the Dunalastair induced other designers to adopt large boilers. Wilson Wordsell's class R 4–4–0 was in service on the North Eastern just before the turn of the century and the Johnson 4–4–0s with Belpaire boilers of the Midland, and Claud Hamiltons of the Great Eastern appeared early in 1900. The large boiler 4–4–0 was thus set to play a major role at the head of twentieth century expresses.

An even bigger locomotive to replace the Stirling singles was being planned by H A Ivatt. In the United States the 4–4–2 Atlantic type was gaining a good reputation for high-speed running and Ivatt built Britain's first Atlantic-type in 1888. It was No 990 *Henry Oakley*, which is preserved in the National Railway Museum. This, his first 4–4–2 design, had a narrow firebox but he followed with a larger boilered Atlantic design which had a wide firebox more akin to the American originals.

Several railways adopted the Atlantic as the logical successor to the 4–2–2 for passenger express work but as train loads increased, the tendency for the driving wheels to slip on wet rails became a problem. The answer came eventually in the use of three coupled axles on the 4–6–0s and 4–6–2 Pacific types, but they did not become common as heavy passenger express engines until well into the twentieth century.

The steam locomotive had made great progress in the second half of the nineteenth century. The GWR's broad-gauge 4–2–2 of 1847 had been brilliant and well ahead of contemporary design but

The traffic into Waterloo, Charing Cross and Victoria at peak commuting periods has always been extremely dense. Electrification was the obvious answer to quick turnround and rapid acceleration. This picture shows an LBSCR tank with a heavy train of close-coupled stock passing under the Brighton line's overhead electrified wires about 1920 but the train is pure Edwardian. (H C Casserley)

the standard-gauge Dunalastair of 1896, with much the same size of boiler and grate, could haul trains of twice the weight at comparable speeds.

While trains had become the accepted means of long-distance travel, they also served for short journeys in towns and cities. New suburbs began to be built beyond centuries-old city boundaries and by the mid-Victorian era workers were no longer living within walking distance of their places of employment. Clerks and artisans and workmen moved out from the centres either into the country or to the edge of the towns where they worked. Some railways around London, particularly the North London, Great Eastern and London, Brighton & South Coast, encouraged the resulting commuter traffic with frequent trains and cheap workmen's fares, though the fare levels, as we have seen, were sometimes imposed by Parliament.

By the early 1900s members of the management echelons commuted daily between the Surrey hills or even the South coast and London. A similar pattern emerged around large provincial cities. The Lancashire & Yorkshire Railway, in particular, ran intensive suburban services into Manchester and senior administrators in the shipping and textile industries travelled from as far as the Lake District and the North Wales coast. They sometimes used first-class-only trains which included club saloons admitting members only. Around Glasgow the Caledonian, the Glasgow & South Western and the North British fought for commuter traffic from the Clyde coast dormitory towns.

The in-town suburban trains continued to have non-corridor compartment coaches – often four-wheeled until World War I – hauled by tank engines which were usually small 0–6–0Ts, 0–4–4Ts or 0–4–2Ts. These were supplemented in the first decade of the twentieth century by larger 0–6–2Ts, or 4–4–2Ts or even larger engines on longer-distance services. On these longer-distance commuter trains corridor coaches were introduced earlier as the commuting habit placed people further from their work.

6
THE GOLDEN YEARS

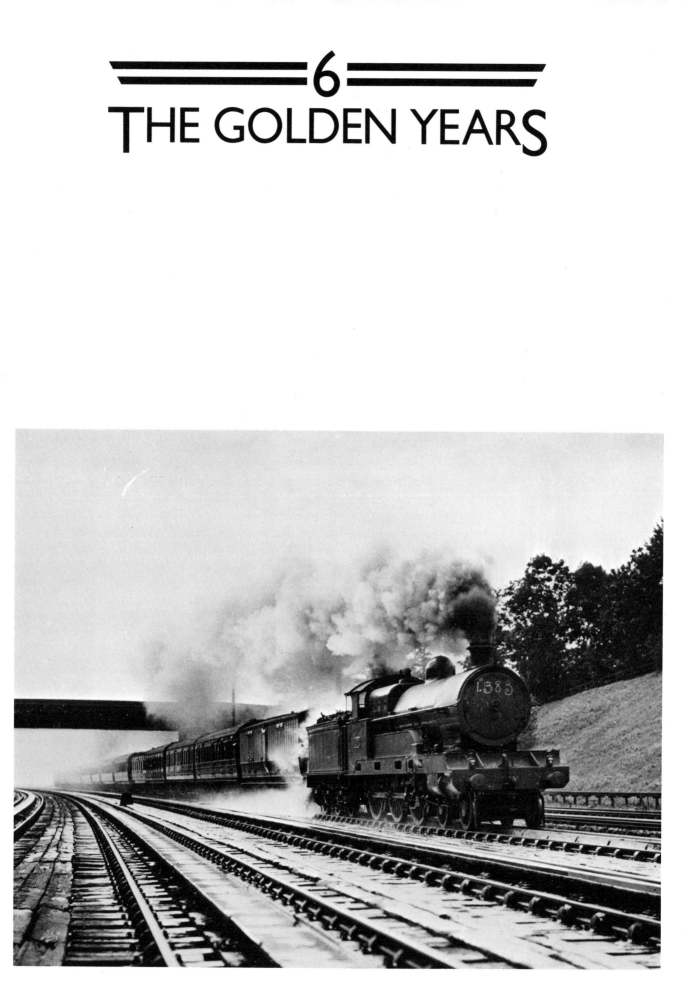

left:
An ex-London & North Western Railway un-named Claughton class 4–6–0 takes water at Bushey heading a 13-coach train. The locomotive is still in LNWR black with its company's cast numberplate and the leading coach is also in its maker's livery of plum and spilt milk. The rest of the train appears to be in the new London Midland & Scottish Railway's red. The date of the photograph is about 1926, just after Grouping. (John Adams)

Class 2 4–4–0 No 405 heads a short Midland Railway express containing typical clerestory coaches which were exceptionally comfortable for their period. Even though this is a post-World War I picture note the cleanliness of the engine with its polished smokebox rim. (P B Whitehouse collection)

The railways of Britain reached their peak in the two decades after the introduction of corridor trains to the outbreak of World War I in 1914. Speeds were higher than before, trains heavier and locomotives more powerful to cope with their extra loads. Electric lighting and steam heating were becoming standard equipment and the internal decor of passenger vehicles was elaborate. Express trains of the period were probably in their most elegant period.

Even so, the first signs of changing conditions which would result in the decline of railways were already appearing. Though the advent of the internal combustion engine towards the end of the nineteenth century did not attract much public attention, by the turn of the century motor vehicles on the roads were becoming a practical proposition. In addition, and more seriously, the development of the electric motor as a means of generating and distributing power had opened the way for electric trams to challenge urban railways for their passenger traffic. In a small way the railways began to use electric power, too, but not yet to any great extent.

Overshadowing all was the growing threat of war which eventually broke in August 1914. The next four years were to impose severe strains on the country's railway system. However, in anticipation of war a Railway Executive Committee was set up in 1912. It consisted of railway general managers and was charged with running the railways as a single co-ordinated system if the need arose. When that need did arise in 1914 the scheme worked well and in only 16 days the railways carried thousands of men, horses and guns of the British Expeditionary Force to Southampton to cross to France. Similarly, plans existed, when war was declared, for the conversion of railway rolling stock to form ambulance trains and by the end of the month 12 such trains were ready.

The Railway Executive Committee controlled 130 railway companies or joint committees and 21,331 route miles. The total railway work force was about 60,000 but more than 30 per cent of employees joined the forces. Shortage of railway staff was by no means the only problem; for example the Highland Railway in particular was overtaxed by the heavy traffic it had to carry for provisioning the Grand Fleet at Scapa Flow. The Executive arranged for it to borrow locomotives from other companies and to have its own engines repaired by outside contractors. In addition the company's locomotive, carriage and wagon superintendent prepared designs for a new 4–6–0 which was to be known as the River class. Sadly, when the first of the six in the class was delivered it was found that its axle-load was too high; the locomotives were useless on that company's lines and were sold to the Caledonian.

Efforts were made during the war to discourage civilian travel, though with little effect, but passenger services were restricted. Even the draconian measures taken in 1917 of abolishing cheap fares and increasing ordinary fares by 50 per cent, with further drastic cuts in services had relatively little effect.

After the Armistice of 11 November 1918 the Government continued outright control of the railways until 15 August 1921. Then

In its early days the LMS was chronically short of express motive power and until the coming of the Royal Scots in 1927 ex-LNWR Claughtons and (as shown here) L & Y 4–6–0s often needed double-heading with anything like a heavy load. This photograph shows ex-LNWR Precursor class No 5263 piloting an unknown L & Y 4–6–0 out of Carlisle. (P B Whitehouse collection)

the Railways Act set out the framework for the wholesale amalgamations of railway companies which became known as the 'Grouping'. In fact, demands for railway nationalisation to consolidate the various useful wartime measures of standardisation and rationalisation under a central body were widespread. However, all-out nationalisation was rejected in favour of the 1921 Act under which 120 railway companies were to be reorganised into four groups from 1 January 1923. The plans for 'Grouping' had been drawn up without any consultation with the companies and various anomalies, such as penetrations by some groups into the territories of others, were enshrined in the Act to the detriment of harmony and full efficiency.

Eight constituents went to make up the largest of the new groups, the London Midland & Scottish Railway (LMS): the London & North Western, the Midland, the Lancashire & Yorkshire, the North Staffordshire, the Caledonian, the Furness, the Glasgow & South Western and the Highland Railways. With 27 subsidiaries, the group had 7500 route miles. The London & North Western and the Lancashire & Yorkshire had worked closely together for years and anticipated the Grouping by amalgamating in January 1922. The LNWR and the Midland also bequeathed to the LMS the Northern Counties Committee and the Dundalk, Newry & Greenore Railway.

above left:
Inside the kitchen of an LMS restaurant car in the early days of Grouping. (C J Allen collection)

above right:
The late 1930s saw the smart Gresley-designed buffet cars on most long-distance excursion and many ordinary trains. (C J Allen collection)

right:
Rivals, LMS Royal Scot No 6115 and LNER Pacific No 2749, at the south end of Carlisle's Citadel station both waiting for their trains from Scotland in 1929. (P M Alexander)

To attempt to cope with the heavy freights working down the old Midland main line, the LMS ordered a class of 2–6–0 + 0–6–2 Garratts from Beyer-Peacock. These were not altogether successful engines and No 4997 is seen here making hard work of a down freight train north of Elstree in July 1933. (John Adams)

As the LMS had been formed from the companies along the West Coast route, so the London & North Eastern Railway group (LNER) came from the East Coast companies. It had seven constituents: the North Eastern, the Great Northern, Great Eastern, Great Central, Hull & Barnsley, North British and the Great North of Scotland. There were 26 subsidiaries and the group had a total mileage of about 6700. Among the companies, the North Eastern and the Hull & Barnsley had merged on 1 January 1922. The Great Central was something of a problem because of its cross-country main line in the north and its London main line; both encroached on LMS territory. But it eventually provided the LNER with a useful relief route between London and the North East.

The only line to remain largely intact was the Great Western, which retained its name and its previous structure. The seven constituents were the GWR itself and, in Wales, the Barry, Cambrian, Rhymney, Taff Valley, Cardiff and the Alexandra (Newport & South Wales) Docks & Railways. It also absorbed 26 subsidiary companies to provide a new route mileage for the GWR of 3800 miles.

The new Southern Railway was the smallest of the groups, with only about 2200 route miles. Its constituents were the London & South Western, the South Eastern, the London, Chatham & Dover and the London, Brighton & South Coast. There were 14 subsidiaries. The SER and LCDR had formed the South Eastern & Chatham Railways Joint Managing Committee on 1 August 1899 to rationalise services and work the lines of both companies. That organisation continued until Grouping.

Although the Southern was small it made up for this with the density of its traffic in south-east England and the sprawling suburban areas of London south of the Thames. Various suburban electrification schemes, which had been in hand at the time of Grouping, were continued and the Southern eventually reached the coast with an electric system. The SECR and LB&SCR brought into the group the relatively short-distance Continental boat trains and the 'Southern

The King of Railway Locomotives – or so said the GWR publicity people. An unknown GWR King class 4–6–0 on Rowington water troughs north of Warwick in 1933. The taking of water at high speed from troughs between the tracks sometimes provided this Niagara Falls effect on the first coach of a train. (P B Whitehouse collection)

above right:
Famous Crossing: A Gresley LNER Pacific No 2570 *Gladiator* leaves Newcastle Central station and is about to enter the complex crossing of tracks *circa* 1927. Note the electrically controlled signal gantry. (National Railway Museum)

Belle' all-Pullman London–Brighton express and the L&SW contributed its main lines to Bournemouth and to the West Country.

Perhaps inevitably, the enforced merging of so many companies brought problems to some of the new groups, though the change went quite smoothly for the Great Western, which was virtually unaffected. On the LMS rivalries between men from the constituent companies caused disruptions which lasted for a decade. The post of Chief Mechanical Engineer went to George Hughes, from the Lancashire & Yorkshire. Policy at the main centres, Crewe, Derby and St Rollox, on the Caledonian, was little changed until his retirement in 1825. Then Sir Henry Fowler, who had been Chief Mechanical Engineer at Derby, took over and immediately began a programme to standardise LMS locomotives. This resulted in a predominance of smaller engines because as older locomotives were made redundant they were replaced with new engines from what were considered the best of the remaining designs. These tended to be from the former Midland Railway, which had favoured small engines. As a result, the LMS operators on the West Coast route, which required large locomotives, felt they were being neglected.

Eventually the LMS ran short of locomotives powerful enough to haul the increasing weight of trains. The need for a new six-coupled design could not be overlooked. In 1926 a Castle class 4–6–0 had been borrowed from the GWR and had performed excellently. An LMS 4–6–0 was quickly designed and the North British Locomotive Company Limited received an order to build 50 of the three-cylinder Royal Scots, as the class was named. In fact, the class performed well and proved themselves more than a mere stop-gap until W A (later Sir William) Stanier was appointed CME in 1932 and began a new era of locomotive design.

The 4–4–0 had been the established express locomotive at the turn of the century, 4–4–2s were being introduced on some lines and the 4–6–0 had just appeared in a few designs of goods or small mixed-traffic engines. However, the 4–6–0 concept was expanded to much larger proportions by J F McIntosh of the Caledonian in 1903 when he built two, No 49 and No 50, which were essentially Dunalastair 4–4–0s expanded into six-couplers. These, which were claimed as Britain's largest and most powerful express locomotives, were overtaken by McIntosh's larger version, the 903 or *Cardean* class. The engine which gave its name to the class, No 903 *Cardean*, worked almost daily on the afternoon express from Glasgow to Euston, running as far as Carlisle and returning on the 'down' express. In 1909 *Cardean* achieved unexpected fame when being tested over the LNWR line between Carlisle and Preston. Running fully extended uphill with a load of 390 tons, it sustained a speed of 44mph up the 1-in-75 gradient of Shap.

Though the early six-coupled engines were much publicised, there was, in truth, little room for further development of the saturated steam engine for express passenger work. When fully extended such an engine was burning coal so fast that it was not only uneconomic but also unreasonable to expect the fireman to sustain the stoking rate. The problem of how to reduce coal consumption had concerned some designers at least since the mid-1880s. On the LNWR Francis Webb had experimented with compounds, hoping that the 're-cycling' of steam was the answer but he had only limited success. His successor, George Whale, replaced the compounds with engines of great simplicity, the most successful being the Precursor class 4–4–0.

The relative scarcity and expensiveness of coal in France had provided the incentive for more intensive work on perfecting the compound. One of the outstanding results was the De Glehn compound Atlantic class which put up magnificent performances on the Nord Railway and also attracted the attention of British designers. One of them was G J Churchward, of the Great Western, who, after looking at the best locomotives of the world, aimed to design one which made use of all their best features. He wanted at least to match the theoretical efficiency of a compound cylinder arrangement by improving the steam expansion ration in simple-cylinder locomotives. To achieve this he used long-lap, long-travel valves (instead of the traditional short-lap, short-travel valves of saturated steam engines). In addition he solved the problem of steam leakage past pistons and valves and perfected a correctly proportioned boiler. He carried out tests on GWR tracks with a four-cylinder Nord-type compound Atlantic and two 4–4–2s of the type used on the Paris–Orleans run. He tested them all against his own two-cylinder simple 4–4–2s and 4–6–0s. All the locomotives exceeded Churchward's aim of a draw-bar pull of two tons at 70mph and the British 4–6–0s proved as fast as the French Atlantics. However, the French compounds provided smoother riding than the 4–6–0s since they had better balancing and four cylinders compared with two outside cylinders taking powerful thrusts from 30-inch piston strokes.

As a result of his experiments Churchward built a four-cylinder Atlantic, *North Star*, which was followed by ten four-cylinder 4–6–0s. Thereafter he built further four-cylinder 4–6–0s, which took over much of the heavy work on West Country main lines. From the name of that first experimental four-cylinder engine the various types which followed were given the class name Star while

An experimental turbine locomotive, the Swedish Ljungstrom locomotive carries express-train headlamps near Elstree on the ex-Midland main line. (P B Whitehouse collection)

right:
Lord Nelson class 4–6–0 No 852 *Sir Walter Raleigh* in the 1930s. (John Adams)

his two-cylinder engines were classed as Saints.

British designers had come to appreciate in the early 1900s that the efficiency of their locomotives was improved either by compounding or by building on the Churchward principle of simple, rationally designed locomotives. Even so, several large 4–6–0s designs had appeared which related to neither solution. These included the large and impressive Sir Sam Fay class on the GCR, the Drummond Paddleboxes on the LSWR and the Hughes four-cylinder 4–6–0s of the L&YR, none of which showed any significant advantages over smaller four-coupled types.

It was a German invention which provided the answer for British designers: the superheating system of Dr Wilhelm Schmidt. Incoming steam was divided to pass through a number of small tubes inserted into a suitably enlarged flue tube in the boiler. Steam could thus be dried and condensation reduced, with the result that a superheated engine used about 25 per cent less coal and water to produce the same performance as a saturated steam engine of the same class.

Henry Fowler designed the Royal Scot 4–6–0 for the LMS and from 1927 until the advent of Stanier's reign from 1933, these were the principle express engines for that system. Later, when fitted with Stanier's taper boiler, their performance was revolutionised, but in 1939 No 6126 was as built and is seen here taking a Liverpool to London train past Edge Hill locomotive depot. (Eric Treacy)

Some classes were transformed by the installation of superheating and gave much superior performances.

Perhaps because his engines were already good, the improvement which superheating gave to Churchward's engines was more modest and he used a moderate superheating system instead of a high temperature one. On the other hand the LNWR went for full, high-temperature superheating and C J Bowen Cooke built a superheated Precursor 4–4–0 in 1910 which was named *George the Fifth*. Thanks to advice from Dr Schmidt, the valve design on this locomotive was bettered only on the GWR and the engine proved to have an almost insatiable appetite for hard work out of all proportion to its size.

Engines of the subsequent *George the Fifth* class regularly hauled trains of 400 tons and more at start-to-stop speeds of 55mph south of Preston and needed no assistance to take loads of up to 400 tons over Shap. Even so, the LNWR introduced express 4–6–0s, culminating in the Claughton class, which was intended to rival the Churchward Stars.

The next step from the 4–6–0 was the 4–6–2 Pacific type. The GWR was the first in the field in Britain with its four-cylinder experimental giant No 111 *The Great Bear*, built at Swindon in 1908. Though this famous engine pointed the way to the future, it was really ahead of its time and because the engineers restricted it to the Paddington–Bristol main line, it never proved itself more useful than either the Star or Saint class of 4–6–0s. Pacifics were not taken seriously until the 1920s. Then, just before Grouping, Nigel Gresley of the GNR built two for express service and Sir Vincent Raven follow-

The LNER Sentinel-Cammel steam railcar *Nettle* at work in the 1930s. This was an experiment in economy but was short-lived. One of the problems with railcars was that, in themselves, with a crew of three and comparatively few passengers they were not really viable but if the service was good enough to attract more passengers than they could carry (for instance on market days) the unit was usually not powerful enough to pull a trailer. (Cecil J Allen collection)

ed with a Pacific for the NER. All were three-cylinder 4–6–2s and were intended as prototypes for new classes. When Gresley was appointed CME of the LNER he chose his Pacific to be a new class.

The Great Western had claimed that *The Great Bear* was 'Britain's largest and most powerful passenger locomotive' and even in 1923, after Gresley's Pacific had appeared, they continued with the claim – this time applying it to the new four-cylinder 4–6–0 *Caerphilly Castle*, which was the first of a long and distinguished line of Castle class engines. The GWR's claim was based on the qualification of *theoretical* tractive effort but the LNER objected, saying that the true criterion of power was boiler size.

In 1924 a GWR Castle and an LNER Pacific were exhibited side by side at the Wembley exhibition and in the following year exchange trials were arranged between the two companies. These proved that the smaller GWR engine did its work on less coal not only on its 'home' lines but also on those of the LNER. Its performance was largely the result of its higher boiler pressure and better valve arrangement, which made the Castles more free-running and economical. The valve gear later became standard for many other locomotive types. Gresley also experimented by increasing boiler pressure from 180lb/sq in to 220 and this was adopted for all new Pacifics. One of these, class A3 No 2750 *Papyrus*, reached a maximum speed of 108mph in trials in 1935.

Claims and counter-claims about the performance of the locomotives of rival groups marked the year 1927 as one of keen competition. Towards the end of 1926 the Southern Railway had built a large four-cylinder 4–6–0, No 850 *Lord Nelson*, which had a tractive effort greater than that of a Castle. The Southern, using the GWR's formula, therefore claimed it had the most powerful passenger locomotive in Britain. It is doubtful if an engine of the class could have beaten a Castle in actual performance at that time. In the summer the GWR replied with an engine which carried the 4–6–0 arrangement to its greatest size in Britain: No 6000 *King George V*. This had a tractive effort of more than 40,000lb and the GWR promptly claimed it as 'Britain's mightiest passenger locomotive'. Subsequently the 30 King class engines gave excellent service, almost to the end of steam and *King George V* became one of the country's most famous locomotives.

Stanier, whose appointment as CME of the LMS we have previously mentioned, joined the company from the Great Western, where he had been principal assistant to Churchward's successor, C B Collett. With the shortage of large locomotives to work the West Coast route in mind, Stanier designed No 6200 *The Princess Royal*, which was really a GWR King expanded into a Pacific. The engine was built in 1933 but the class did not achieve complete success until 1935, by which time they had been turned into powerful and efficient locomotives.

While most attention and publicity was centred on the design and performance of express passenger locomotives, it was the workhorses of the railways, the goods and mixed-traffic engines, which earned a large portion of the revenue. Fast goods and secondary passenger services were handled on the lines of all four groups in the 1920s by the 2–6–0 Moguls. However, in 1924 the GWR's 4–6–0 *Saint Martin* was rebuilt with driving wheels of 6ft 0in instead of 6ft 8in. This locomotive ushered in the modern mixed-traffic 4–6–0 type, the intention of the rebuilding being to increase pulling power at moderate speeds without detracting from possible maximum pace. Its success led to the building of the first of the GWR Hall class in 1928.

Passenger traffic and fast express trains may have had the glory but the nitty gritty of railway business has always been freight. This non-glamorous side sometimes gets neglected pictorially but the motive power was there in profusion and a great deal if it was of considerable interest and antiquity.

A 'Great North of Scotland' 0–4–2T as LNER No 8191 shunts fish vans at Aberdeen harbour in 1947. (H C Casserley)

This class eventually totalled 330 engines which could be relied upon to complete virtually any task on the GWR.

In the 1930s William Stanier produced the first of his class 5 4–6–0s, the famous 'Black Fives', for the LMS. The class reached a total of 842 locomotives, a reliable measure of their success. After nationalisation in 1948 the Stanier design was used as the basis for the BR standard 73000 class of 172 engines.

Nigel Gresley, on the LNER, had different ideas about engine size and produced the very large 2–6–2s of the V2 or Green Arrow class. Able to handle the work of Pacifics, they carried out important duties hauling trains of up to 20 coaches in World War II. With an axle-load of 22 tons, they were restricted to main-line work but Gresley designed two smaller 2–6–2s, the Bantam Cock class, to handle secondary traffic. These sturdy engines could run almost anywhere. Shortly after they first had entered service Sir Nigel, as he then was, died. His successor was Edward Thompson, who preferred a two-cylinder 4–6–0 design. His first of this type was the LNER B1 class, which appeared in 1942. The class eventually numbered 410 and the engines gave a performance similar to that of the rival GWR and LMS 4–6–0s.

The majority of goods work was handled by 0–6–0s except for the very heavy duties, when 0–8–0s or 2–8–0s took over. Though the 'goods engine' reached its maximum size between the wars, maximum efficiency was not developed until the appearance of the standard BR 9F 2–10–0 in 1953.

Short-distance and suburban work was undertaken by the tank engines though at one time it seemed that these would also be used extensively on express work over medium-length journeys. Large express tank engines of the 4–6–4T Baltic type (really, self-contained 4–6–0s) were built by several companies but none proved particularly outstanding. The GWR used 2–6–2Ts for its local services and on other lines the 2–6–4T was employed on mixed traffic duties. After

below right:
An unusual engine – in the form of an ex-LSWR railcar unit – 0–4–0T No 30589 runs down the road at Southampton docks in 1949. (P M Alexander)

below:
GWR No 2541 shunts at Kinnersley yard on the daily pick up from Hereford to Brecon. (P M Alexander)

A train on the 2ft 6in gauge Welshpool & Llanfair section of the GWR. Lasting into BR days this line now operates as a tourist railway. This picture shows a freight train nearing Welshpool. (P B Whitehouse)

the derailment of a Southern Railway River class 2–6–4T at Sevenoaks in 1927 the type was mistrusted for a time but was later used extensively by the LMS, achieving maximum speeds of over 80mph.

An indication of the great improvement in engine design can be gained from the fact that between 1900 and 1939 the steam locomotive had doubled its maximum horsepower with only a 30 per cent increase in weight. It had also reduced its coal consumption per unit of work measured at the drawbar by about 40 per cent. Even so, it was still wasteful on fuel and high on maintenance costs. There were already rival forms of power threatening the dominance of the steam locomotive: the GWR was using diesel railcars on some branch and cross-country services; the LMS had diesel shunting engines; and the Southern was pressing ahead with electrification.

After the end of World War I the railways took some time to return to the pre-war standards of express passenger train speeds. The exception was the Great Western, which seemed to have kept its engines well enough maintained to be able to restore 1914 timings on its principal routes from Paddington by 1921. But on most routes there were gaps in the timings between the fast trains and other services. Even after Grouping in 1923 standards remained erratic because locomotives had still not been restored to top condition after the war years of minimum maintenance and over-work. To boost the tarnished image, the railway companies sometimes selected a train for special treatment, naming it and improving its timings.

Though Anglo-Scottish timings remained, until the early 1930s, subject to the agreement reached after the 'great races' of 1888/95, the LMS and LNER still competed for glory in other ways. Long non-stop runs were the most effective form of competition and on 27 April 1928 the LMS stole the LNER's thunder by running the 'Royal Scot' train in two parts non-stop from Euston to Glasgow and Edinburgh respectively three days before the LNER 'Flying Scotsman' began non-stop running between Kings Cross and Edinburgh. However, the LMS could not produce such runs to schedule whereas the 'Flying Scotsman' went on to claim and retain the world record for length of regular daily non-stop working.

Despite growing competition on the roads in the early 1930s, the train remained the most convenient means of travel and any national event was sure to attract and fill several excursion trains. In the summer the main-line routes to the coast were packed with so many extra trains that freight traffic and often local passenger services were curtailed. On Saturdays the GWR's 'Cornish Riviera' express, normally a single train, often had to run in as many as four parts, leaving at five-minute intervals.

The GWR also laid claim to run 'the fastest train in the world' when it raised the average speed between Swindon and Paddington to over 70mph of a lightweight and previously insignificant Cheltenham–London express, which became known as 'The Cheltenham Flyer'. There were moves elsewhere to capture new traffic and the LNER aimed at the luxury end of the market with new Pullman trains between Kings Cross and Yorkshire and with the 'Queen of Scots' to Glasgow. The Southern brought in new Pullman services for Bournemouth and for the 'Golden Arrow' between London and the Channel ports.

The Southern Railway inherited the 2ft 0in gauge Lynton & Barnstaple Railway in 1923. Never an economic reality the section was closed in 1935. Here is the American-built Baldwin tank No 762 *Lyn* leaving Barnstaple in 1934. (D E H Box)

In steam days the use of pusher or banker engines to assist the train engine when climbing steep inclines was very much the rule. This was particularly the case with heavy freight trains.
Three LMS engines No 7638, No 7308 and No 3433 help a heavy freight to ascend the Lickey incline from Bromsgrove. (H C Casserley)

The railways were now also having to take steps to counter the growing competition from buses and motorcoaches which were able to link villages with urban centres, often at much lower fares. Fast cross-country and outer-suburban trains were introduced by the LNER. These included Kings Cross–Cambridge, Newcastle–Carlisle, Leeds–Scarborough and Hull–Liverpool. Buffet cars, which the LNER used widely on secondary services were included in some of these trains.

Once again passenger accommodation came in for attention and improvement by the designers. In 1927 the LMS introduced a new type of coach which did away with compartment doors and was the forerunner of today's inter-city carriage. At first these were only used for first-class travel but by the start of the 1930s they were also available as third-class accommodation. First-class coaches for the 'Royal Scot' and other named expresses were laid out for just four passengers, two either side, in compartments which were well-upholstered and had wide picture windows. The LNER also brought out two-a-side first-class coaches in its improved coach sets for the 'Flying Scotsman'. Restaurant cars were furnished in Louis XIV style with free-moving armchairs, concealed lighting and hand-painted decor. In the adjoining kitchen cars Gresley, who pioneered electric cooking on trains in Britain, had installed electric refrigerators.

Built for the accelerated services to Scotland in the late 1930s, Stanier's 4–6–2 Duchess class Pacifics were very successful engines. The streamlined versions were painted in blue and silver or, as with No 6225 *Duchess of Gloucester* seen here passing through Rugby, in red and gold. (P B Whitehouse collection)

All but the Southern introduced third-class sleeping cars in the late 1920s. Previously only first-class passengers had night berths; third-class passengers were given only a pillow and a rug.

Open-plan coaches were introduced not only because they carried more passengers but also because they were thought to appeal to third-class passengers by resembling the interior of road motor-coaches. At first only the LMS and LNER used them; the GWR regarded them, loftily, as only suitable for excursion trains and, other than as dining cars, barred them from scheduled services. The SR included part-open saloon accommodation in its express electric units.

The end of the 1930s saw the railways attaining new peaks in terms of public interest in the feats of express trains, even if not in terms of financial returns. In the face of increasing competition from road vehicles, air transport, diesel and electric traction, it seemed as though the steam locomotive was making a final determined bid to retain its supremacy. Part of that bid came in the form of the dramatic streamliners, with LNER leading the way. After high-speed trials in 1934 with improved Gresley A3 Pacifics, during which No 4472 reached the first undisputed 100mph in Britain and a sister engine 108mph a few months later, the LNER introduced a new train on a four-hour timing to Newcastle in the autumn of 1935. The train was named 'Silver Jubilee' in honour of King George V's 25 years on the throne and it was fully streamlined. In particular the silver-grey livery and the distinctive shape of Gresley's Pacific attracted attention. The wedge-shaped nose helped to carry smoke and steam clear of the cab windows apart from other aerodynamic considerations. However, underneath the streamlining the new A4 was not much different from the non-streamlined A3 Pacific, though slightly more powerful. In ordinary daily service the 'Silver Jubilee' could maintain only a maximum speed of 90mph, even though on a demonstration run in September 1935 it covered 70 miles at 90mph, 25 miles at 107mph and reached a peak of 112.5mph. However, in daily service it was still much faster than any other British train over comparable distances and an hour was cut from the previous journey time.

The 'Silver Jubilee's' success was followed with demands for a similar service to Edinburgh but the LMS would have preferred to concentrate generally on improving all services rather than introducing one crack express. Even so, when a high-speed service to Edinburgh was mooted, the LMS had to protect its Glasgow service. After trials with Princess Pacific No 6201, which had worked an eight-coach set from Glasgow to Edinburgh in $5\frac{3}{4}$ hours, the LMS introduced a high-speed train to Glasgow in the summer of 1937, using a larger streamlined Pacific. In view of the test performance by No 6201 *Princess Elizabeth*, the schedule of $6\frac{1}{2}$ hours set for this new 'Coronation Scot' train was considered unduly cautious, particularly when compared with the LNERs proposal to run its 'Coronation' express to Edinburgh in six hours.

The first LMS streamlined Pacific, No 6220, was also named *Coronation* and it had a slightly larger boiler than the LNER's A4. Though the gradients on the West Coast route were steeper than on the East, the locomotives were well matched in terms of speed and capability. Aerodynamically the rounded streamlining of the nose of the *Coronation* might have been better than the wedge of the A4 but it did not carry smoke and steam away from the cab as effectively. Engine and coach set were painted blue with silver lines extending from the front of the engine to the rear brake van. The LNER A4s for the 'Coronation' train were also blue with red wheels, while the coaches had Marlborough blue on the top half and Garter blue below.

The LMS *Coronation* left Euston on 29 June 1937 for a demonstration run of the 'Coronation Scot' to Crewe and back. Naturally the company did not want to be left out of the publicity which the LNER had gained when *Silver Link* had reached 112.5mph for the LNER, followed by 113mph by *Silver Fox* in 1936. Unfortunately, the LMS had no stretch of line as suitable as the LNER's Stoke Bank and had to be content with the descent to Crewe from Whitmore. That, however, left precious little distance in which to stop the train from a high speed.

After passing Stafford *Coronation* was opened out and passed Whitmore at 85mph. Speed built up rapidly and near milepost 156 it was estimated on stop watches to be 113mph – the same as *Silver Fox*. But the locomotive's speedometer recorded 114mph and, despite the possibility of inaccuracy, the record was claimed by the

LMS. *Coronation* was still accelerating when steam was shut off and the train had just two miles to run into Crewe station. Flames were seen coming from the brake blocks as the train slowed rapidly, rattling alarmingly over points and sending crockery flying before halting safely at platform 3.

Although the record went to the LMS it had to be acknowledged that the LNER's 'Coronation' train was the more exciting in general performance. The 'Coronation Scot' could keep time with maximum speeds of no higher than 83–85mph; the 'Coronation' travelled at up to 90mph and occasionally went over 100mph to a top recorded speed of 107mph. The daily booking of 157 minutes, start-to-stop, from Kings Cross to York was the fastest ever recorded for steam in Britain.

A third streamliner was added by the LNER in the autumn of 1937 with the 'West Riding Limited' from Kings Cross to Leeds. The LMS did not introduce any similar trains for the London to Manchester or Liverpool service and instead made all-round improvements to the speed and frequency of ordinary services.

It was these two long-time rivals who figured in the peaks of achievement by British steam locomotives in the last two years of

Gresley's one time *Hush Hush* high-pressure 4–6–4 as rebuilt and streamlined at Kings Cross in 1939. (Colourviews Picture Library)

peace. While carrying out brake tests down Stoke Bank on 3 July 1938 the LNER A4 Pacific No 4468 *Mallard*, hauling 240 tons, reached a sustained speed of 125mph and peak of 126mph. Although the speeds were attained downhill, this was a world record for steam and *Mallard* was a smaller engine than others in the United States and Germany which had achieved over 120mph.

The LMS record was not one of speed but of power. In February 1939 the non-streamlined Pacific No 6234 *Duchess of Abercorn* ran on the Crewe–Glasgow main line with 20 coaches weighing 610 tons. A drawbar horsepower of over 2500 was recorded in the dynamometer car and the officially calculated indicated horsepower in the cylinders was over 3500. This, too, was a British record and both performances remain unsurpassed by steam.

The two locomotives, *Mallard* and *Duchess of Abercorn*, each had double chimneys, which improved their performances in two ways: by permitting better draughting, which raised more steam, and by reducing back pressure because exhaust steam escaped more freely. The double chimney was later used to good purpose in reducing coal consumption during and after the war which was effectively to put an end to the golden years of steam.

During the last five years of the 1930s there was considerable competition for passengers' favours over the West Coast route to Scotland (LMS) and the East Coast route (LNER). Both companies used forms of streamlined trains and distinctive liveries. Here is the LNER's 'Coronation' express crossing the Royal Border Bridge at Berwick. The engine is a Gresley A4 Pacific in Garter blue. Note the beavertail observation coach at the rear of the train. (E R Wethersett)

Oliver Bulleid's controversial Merchant Navy and West Country Pacifics were the Southern's last express engines. With encased chain-driven valve gear and thermic syphons, these engines were of a startling design. Later in the BR days, many were rebuilt under the expert eye of R G Jarvis as more conventional machines.

Merchant Navy class 4–6–2 No 35010 *Blue Star* in ex-works condition and green livery heads the down 'Bournemouth Belle' on 4 April 1953. (P M Alexander)

Nameplate Merchant Navy class No 35016. (Colourviews Picture Library)

The outbreak of World War II on 3 September 1939 was not unexpected and plans for centralised control of the railways in readiness for mass movement of troops, military equipment and civilian evacuation had been prepared during the previous 12 months. Two days before the formal declaration of war the Government took control of the four main-line railways as well as the London Passenger Transport Board and five minor railways. As in World War I, this action was taken through a Railway Executive Committee which on this occasion was made up by the general managers of the four main railways and of the LPTB. The executive had its headquarters in a disused tube station in the heart of London but those of the main-line railways were moved to various country mansions in the first weekend of September.

The first four days of the war saw the successful completion of one of the most remarkable mass passenger transport movements in all railway history: over 600,000 civilians (most of them children) were evacuated from London in 1577 special trains and more than 700,000 others from 17 other major centres of population in England and Scotland were moved out in a further 2246 trains.

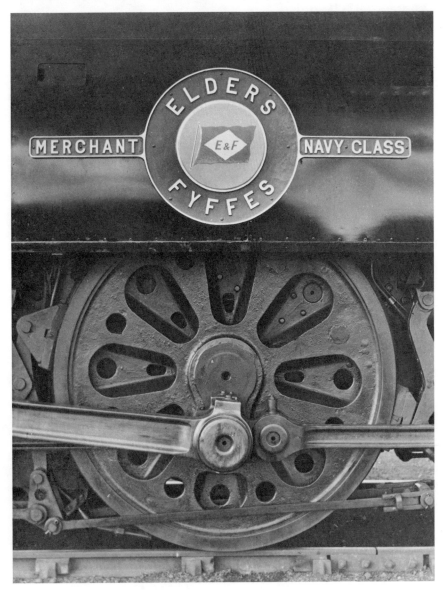

Both World Wars had required locomotives for military use in Europe and the Middle East. In World War I the army made use of existing types. World War II also conformed to this pattern with selected classes (for example, the GWR Dean Goods 0–6–0s and the Stanier 2–8–0s) but new classes were also built both in the UK and the USA. The UK engines comprised three classes designed by Riddles, a 2–8–0 and a 2–10–0 tender engine and an 0–6–0 saddle tank; the USA engines were 2–8–0s and 0–6–0 tanks.

Ex-Midland Railway 0–6–0 as Railway Operating Department No 2727 awaits disposal at Derby works in 1920 after use by the War Department. (H C Casserley)

Ex-LBSCR I2 class 4–4–2T as WD No 72401 stands forlornly at Guildford in January 1949 after use on the Longmoor Military Railway, Hants. (P M Alexander)

A US Army transportation Corps 2–8–0 No 1833 waits at Leicester Central towards the end of the war. (A W Flowers)

Unlettered with regard to ownership and with an undecipherable number, an 'Austerity' 2–8–0, built for the Government during the war, trundles a freight between Widney Manor and Knowle & Dorridge on 24 April 1948. (C F H Oldham)

Once again the passenger service was drastically curtailed and timings slowed down. In some cases journey times were even longer than at the height of World War I. Throughout the railway system speed limits were operated to conserve fuel and reduce maintenance needs. The famous named expresses and streamliners were taken off 'for the duration' and, as it transpired, the latter never returned. In 1940, after the deceptive calm of the 'phoney war', the railways were called upon to become involved in the military operation of the evacuation of Dunkirk. Between 27 May and 4 June nearly 300,000 British soldiers who had been rescued off the beaches of Dunkirk were transported from the Channel ports in 565 special trains, of which 327 ran from Dover. Having expected to have to cope with only about 30,000 men, the railway staff carried through a feat of improvisation which was extraordinary as well as unique. A further 200 special trains were laid on early in June to carry survivors from the western ports of France to reception areas which had been set up in the West Country.

A Great Central C14 class 4–4–2T
No 67442 on the old Cambrian/
Great Western system at Oswestry
in May 1949. This was the Wrexham-
Oswestry auto service and the trailer
car is GWR. The 4–4–2T was a
Wrexham engine from the GCR/
LNER-controlled Wrexham Mold &
Connors Quay line of pre-
nationalisation days. (P M Alexander)

During the final years of 1947 the
railways turned towards
experimentation with oil firing.
These two ex-LSWR T9 class
4–4–0s, stand outside the shed at
Eastleigh in September 1947. (H C
Casserley)

The Dunkirk railway operation served as a dramatic warning of the
sort of pressure under which the system was soon going to have to
operate. Not only were the railways called upon to carry a mounting
burden of freight traffic and to muster extremely long passenger
and goods trains, they also became targets for the German bombers.
Although the number of passenger trains had been reduced and
civilians were again urged not to travel – 'Is your journey really
necessary?' was a slogan of the time – thousands of military personnel
were daily being transported about the country. The extra numbers
generated huge trains and on the East Coast main line at least one
25-coach train was run from Kings Cross.

The pressure on freight services rose dramatically, not so much in
terms of numbers of trains as in the need for more efficient loading, a
loss of staff to the Forces and a decline in the standard of rolling stock
because of the impossibility of keeping up with maintenance requirements. The traditional movement of much freight by night had to
continue but now, because of the blackout, it was done with the

Many pre-Grouping classes were saved from earlier extinction by the onset of World War II. Here are two such engines, now on secondary work and with only a short time to go before scrapping.

Watford Junction station with a semi-fast train from Euston to Bletchley. The engine is a LNWR Prince of Wales class 4–6–0 No 25752 in September 1946. (H C Casserley)

Nottingham's Victoria station with ex-GNR D class 4–4–0 with a branch train for Grantham in July 1947. (H C Casserley)

minimum of light. Despite all these difficulties net ton mileage had risen 43 per cent by 1943 compared with peacetime levels. This was achieved in spite of the intensive attacks on the railways by German bombers, principally in the 'Blitz' of 1940–41 but also with the V1 'doodle-bug' flying bombs and the V2 rockets. As soon as damage to railway property – particularly the permanent way and signalling – was reported, 'flying squads' of railwaymen were rushed to the scene to carry out immediate repairs, often working while air raids continued around them and bombs still fell.

As the tide of the war changed, the railways became involved in the RAF's preparation for the day-and-night air offensive against German targets. The massive construction programme for 150 new bomber airfields in East Anglia and new fighter bases in Kent and Sussex meant that the railways had, first, to carry the building materials to country stations near each site and then, once the bases were ready for occupation, transport the personnel. The LNER estimated that it had run 460 special trains to take the men to the

During the late 1950s attempts were made to individualise the various regions of BR as far as liveries were concerned – some LMR express engines were repainted red, Liverpool Street station had a blue station pilot and the Western Region went back to chocolate and cream for its coaching stock. It was smart, evocative and nostalgic, but new colours did not reduce the deficit!

left:
Clouds tower over the east-bound 'Merchant Venturer' as it approaches Chippenham, Wiltshire. (G F Heiron)

bottom:
Foreigner at work. A surprised car driver stares at LMS Duchess class Pacific No 46236 *City of Bradford* near Sidmouth Junction Southern Region during the locomotive 'Exchange Trials' on 24 June 1948. (C F H Oldham)

below:
The driver watches from his cab for the green light as rebuilt Merchant Navy class No 35030 *Elder Dempster Lines* waits to head out of Waterloo with the 'Atlantic Coast Express' bound for Exeter and Ilfracombe. (G F Heiron)

left:
On the formation of British Railways it was deemed necessary to show unity as soon as possible by means of standard liveries for engines and coaches. In the event the most powerful passenger engines were painted blue (short-lived), lesser express engines GWR green, mixed traffic engines lined out black and others plain black. Here is *Coronation* class Pacific No 46248 *City of Leeds* in blue livery moving the fully loaded 15-coach 'Mid-day Scot' out of Euston station, bound for Glasgow. (G F Heiron)

During the mid-1950s the London Midland Region of BR took over the GWR-owned Cambrian section and almost immediately replaced ex-Great Western engines with BR standards! Here is the up 'Cambrian Coast Express' climbing Talerddig bank behind the standard class 4 No 75005 in April 1956. (P B Whitehouse)

BR class 5 4–6–0 No 73081 leaves Dumpton Park with a morning train from Ramsgate to London in June 1959. (P B Whitehouse)

below:
A South Wales named express – the 'Red Dragon' – races down the main line near Challow behind No 70029. (J F Russell Smith)

The Britannias were intended as BR's answer to the second line express engine of the future – and so they were under suitable conditions. They revolutionised the London (Liverpool Street) to Norwich service, they made more than a good mark on the Southern's 'Golden Arrow' and even the aloof Western Region took them to their hearts – albeit with ex-GWR names.

No 70020 with the good Western name of *Mercury* storms out of Patchway tunnel with the up 'Capitals Express' (Cardiff–London) in May 1959. (G F Heiron)

East Anglian bases. Nor was that the end of the requirement, for when the air operations got under way the railways carried the munitions and fuel. A thousand-bomber raid required 28 fuel trains and eight bomb-carrying trains.

The greatest pressure of all came from the D-Day invasion and the build-up to it. From 26 March 1944 until the start of the invasion offensive on 6 June the railways had to run 24,459 special trains. In the week before D-Day there were 3636 extra trains to be scheduled, and in the four weeks after D-Day the demands became even more severe with the need to maintain essential supplies, carry forces' mail, lay on ambulance trains and carry incoming prisoners of war. The special train total in the four weeks after D-Day rose to over 18,000.

When the war ended in 1945 the railways were near breaking point and materially exhausted, with stock run down to the barest mini-

Waterloo station one year into nationalisation. On the right is a Lord Nelson class 4–6–0. (C J Allen collection)

mum and in desperate need of maintenance or replacement. The LMS calculated that £14 million was needed to catch up on arrears of maintenance on its tracks and signalling equipment and a further £26 million to bring the track back to acceptable peacetime standards. But that sort of money was not available to the railways, whose finances had been severely drained even before the war by the slump of the 1930s coupled with the drop in freight traffic because of competition from lorries. They had also invested heavily before the war in express passenger equipment. In 1938 only the GWR had been able to pay shareholders a dividend; the LNER's investors had received no return on their shares for four years. To add to their economic problems the Government failed to live up to its promise to reimburse the railways adequately for their work during the war. Indeed, the railways' revenue, which by 1942 was twice the annual payment of £43 million received from the Government, had been retained by Whitehall so that by 1945 the companies had actually lost money to the Government.

Stanier's ubiquitous 'Black Five' class 4–6–0 was probably one of Britain's most successful locomotives. They were seen hard at work from Bristol to Wick and gave particularly good service (often double-headed) on the main line to the old Highland Railway from Perth to Inverness. (W J V Anderson)

above right:
West Highland shed: Fort William Loco depot in 1953. Note that all engines are ex-LNER with a predominance of Gresley's K2 class 2–6–0s specially named for use on the West Highland line in the 1920/30s. Also on shed are ex-NBR Glen class 4–4–0s used in tandem with the 2–6–0s on most heavy trains. (P B Whitehouse)

When a Labour Government was returned in 1945 it became inevitable that, despite a vigorous campaign by the four companies, the railways would be nationalised. Though several senior officers chose early retirement rather than work for an all-embracing Government-controlled system, the majority of railway employees greeted nationalisation with delight. The 1947 Transport Act covered all forms of transport and aimed at a co-ordinated system – an ideal that was not achieved. The British Transport Commission which took over on 1 January 1948 was established as corporate overlord of subordinate Transport Executives responsible for day-to-day management of main-line railways, public road transport, docks, canals, and London Transport.

As in the Grouping operation after World War I, the GWR again suffered little physical alteration; nor did the Southern. They were changed to the Western and Southern Regions. However, the LMS and LNER were considered too long and widespread to be controlled as two Regions. Both surrendered their territory north of the

Waverley station, the Scottish terminus of the East Coast route, built by the North British Railway as it was in the early 1960s almost unchanged for over half a century. On the left is Edinburgh's Princes Street, whilst the great edifice of the North British Hotel towers over the station itself. Ex-NBR locomotives can be seen on the left and right, whilst the express in the centre is hauled by an A1 Pacific. (Eric Treacy)

During its latter days of operation engines of Southern and LMS parentage were seen hard at work on passenger trains over the Somerset & Dorset Joint Railway. The Southern provided the light Bulleid Pacifics of the West County class and the LMS numerous class 2P 4–4–0s as pilots. Here is Masbury Summit in August 1952 with ex-LMS 2P No 40696 piloting West Country Pacific No 34042 *Dorchester* over the 1 in 50 gradient. (P M Alexander)

border to the new Scottish Region; the LMS in the south became the London Midland Region and the LNER was divided into the Eastern and the North Eastern Regions. (In 1967 they were re-united into a single Eastern Region based at York.) The power vested in the pre-war railway management was not transferred to the new regional headquarters. Instead the Railway Executive exercised strict control from boardroom to 'track level' in every department.

Despite notable advances made in diesel traction in Germany and North America, the new Railway Executive made the momentous decision to continue with steam traction. Although after the war the LMS and LNER had decided to mount pilot main-line dieselisation schemes, only the LMS had actually started when the Railway Executive decided to develop a new range of standard, mainly mixed-traffic steam locomotives in seven power ranges up to express passenger Pacific status. One was a heavy freight class 9 2–10–0, the only earlier equivalent of which had been a wartime austerity design. In fact the class 9 was used on fast passenger trains on occasions.

LNER streamliners: Gresley built his famous A4s after a visit to Germany to see the 'Flying Hamburger' during the mid-1930s. These most successful engines were used for the streamlined 'Silver Jubilee' and 'Coronation' expresses as well as for other principal express trains after 1935. In BR days A4 Pacific No 60028 *Walter K Whigham* hauls the 1950s 'Elizabethan' to a magnificent crescendo of sound as it streaks out of Hadley Wood terminal at 80mph. (G F Heiron)

The familiar sound of a hard working GWR engine echoes across the Golden Valley as a Cheltenham – Paddington express climbs the final 1 in 60 gradient to Sapperton tunnel in Gloucestershire. (G F Heiron)

During the early days of nationalisation and before steam became a dirty word, numerous experiments were carried out with locomotives belonging to the old companies to attempt to evaluate results for future progress. Here is an LNER V2 2–6–2 ('Green Arrow' class) under trials on the Western Region during the 1950s using the old GWR Dynamometer car. (P M Alexander)

On branch lines carrying sparse traffic it was sometimes necessary to combine passenger and freight trains. This practice was more common in the older days but even as late as 1949 and into the 1950s it appertained to th the old North Devon & Cornwall Junction Light Railway – a section of the Southern from Halwill Junction to Torrington. Here is an LBSCR E1/R class 0–6–2T on Marland viaduct, Torrington, with a mixed train from Halwill in May 1949. (P M Alexander)

The LMS, in its preparation for the pilot scheme, had produced two prototype 1600hp main-line diesel-electric engines in 1947 and in the early 1950s the Southern Region was authorised to build three more, while the Western, ever striving for some measure of independence, experimented with two gas turbine-electric locomotives, one of which was British and the other Swiss.

Britain was the only Western country to commit itself so heavily to steam in the post-war era. The decision lost British Railways the chance for orderly evaluation of various designs of diesel before steam was phased out and resulted in the costly and hectic rush into dieselisation with a variety of largely untried designs a few years later. The dogmatic attitude was one reason for the very slow progress made in Britain towards achieving the pre-war standards of train service. There was a serious shortage of good steam coal and, in addition, the attractiveness of a secure job on the railways which had been there before the war was diminished by the availability of many

When the Southern Railway electrified its main line (the old LSWR route) to Portsmouth it was not worth its while to deal likewise with the country branches *en route*. Here is Petersfield Junction in June 1951 with an LSWR M7 class 0–4–4 tank and push-and-pull train leaving from the little Midhurst branch platform which was on the opposite side of the level crossing from the main station. (P M Alexander)

The 'Norseman' departs from Kings Cross terminus behind A3 class Pacific No 60054 *Prince of Wales* *circa* 1950. (G F Heiron)

new, cleaner and better-paid employment opportunities. As a result steam depot staffs dropped below the official establishment level and there was a corresponding drop in maintenance.

In the final years of their independence the four major companies had embarked on steam construction programmes. The Southern had introduced new classes during the war with the attempt by its Chief Mechanical Engineer, O V S Bulleid to adapt the steam locomotive to the changing conditions. He came up with a new 4–6–2 design in which he combined a boiler of high steam-raising capacity with three cylinders and a chain-driven valve gear running in a closed oil bath. Rather than streamlining he employed 'air smoothing' by encasing the engine in metal sheeting – the intention as much as anything, being to save labour by cleaning the engines in carriage washing plants.

The first Bulleid 4–6–2 of 1941 was classed as a mixed-traffic type, to avoid a wartime ban on the construction of any passenger loco-motives. The type proved capable of the highest speeds required and was produced in two classes, the large engines being named after Merchant Navy themes and the second, smaller and lighter engines bearing West Country and Battle of Britain names. In subsequent

A pair of ex-North London Railway 0–6–0 tanks, kept specially to work the upper section of the Cromford and High Peak line wait at Middleton top before ascending the notorious Hopton incline. (P B Whitehouse)

BR re-building the air-smoothing was removed. All new LMR Pacifics were built without streamlining. Only the Gresley A4s were allowed to survive as streamliners.

Railway operating methods in the first few years after nationalisation continued much as before and in many respects there might have seemed to have been few changes since the steam age was at its height. The variety of the loads carried by mixed freight trains continued to reflect the principle laid down in the Railway and Canal Traffic Act of 1854 of 'obligation to carry' all articles offered for transportation. Just as in pre-war days, most stations still had their goods shed and sidings which received at least a daily visit from a goods train. The transport of minerals – the reason that the Stockton and Darlington had been built in 1825 – remained an important revenue earner and in fact in the 125 years to 1950 the annual tonnage of coal carried by rail was well over half the total volume of freight. When the railways were nationalised in 1948 there were more than 600,000 privately owned wagons in use and most of these passed to British Railways. Whereas they had previously been used for the owners' purposes they now became available for multi-purpose use. However, there was a limiting factor in that many of the wagons

Ex-London and South Western Railway signals at Mount Pleasant in 1951. Note the ringed arms denoting slow or goods lines. (P M Alexander)

right:
Odd corners of the British Railways system remained almost unchanged well into the late 1950s. One such period piece was the part adhesion (over viciously sharp curves) part rope-worked Cromford & High Peak section of the LMR in Derbyshire. This view is up the lower incline from Cromford Wharf in 1961. (G D King)

were not fitted with power brakes controlled by the driver; most had mechanical handbrakes which were applied individually by shunters running alongside wagons and using poles to manipulate the brakes. The wagons with vacuum power brakes were mainly used to carry perishable goods on freight express trains. Trains without the advantage of controlled power braking throughout had to stop or slow to a crawl so that the handbrakes could be applied and pinned in the 'on' position, or else they relied only on the steam brake-power of the engine and the handbrake in the guard's van.

The situation was not really resolved in the early days after nationalisation because the British Transport Commission had hardly got to grips with the complexities of evolving a co-ordinated transport system before the General Election of 1952 put a Conservative Government in power. The Transport Act of 1953 not only de-nationalised much of the road transport industry but also began the abolition of BR's statutory charging and 'common carrier' obligations. This led the way to the market pricing and freedom to reject traffic which exist today. The Act also abolished the Executives and gave full responsibility for running the railways to the British Transport Commission. It was, however, a very rundown railway system, even though some services were getting back to pre-war standards.

An ex-LBSCR C2X class 0–6–0 on the Chichester to Midhurst branch in 1951 – at that time the only service over the line was this daily freight. (P M Alexander)

above:
The 'Red Dragon'
(Colourviews
Picture Library)

below:
Ex-GWR No 4080 *Powderham Castle*,
fitted with a double chimney to
improve steaming with the poorer
coal then available, heads a London
(Paddington) express in 1961.
(Colourviews Picture Library)

British Railways standard Britannia class 4–6–2 No 70025 *Western Star* with a mixed freight near Badminton in 1961. (Colourviews Picture Library)

above:
Drem Junction in June 1972 with the
1516 hours London to Edinburgh
express behind Deltic D7017 *The
Durham Light Infantry*. (Derek Cross)

left:
Newcastle Central station, Eastern
Region in March 1970. This train
carrying cars bound for the north is
hauled by Type 4 diesel-electric
locomotive of class 40, No D.274.
(Derek Cross)

EMU No 313.059 comes out of the
tunnel into Hadley Wood Station
on its way to London Moorgate,
using the up fast line due to
engineering works, June 1978.
(Peter Howard)

=8=
NEW FORMS OF PROPULSION

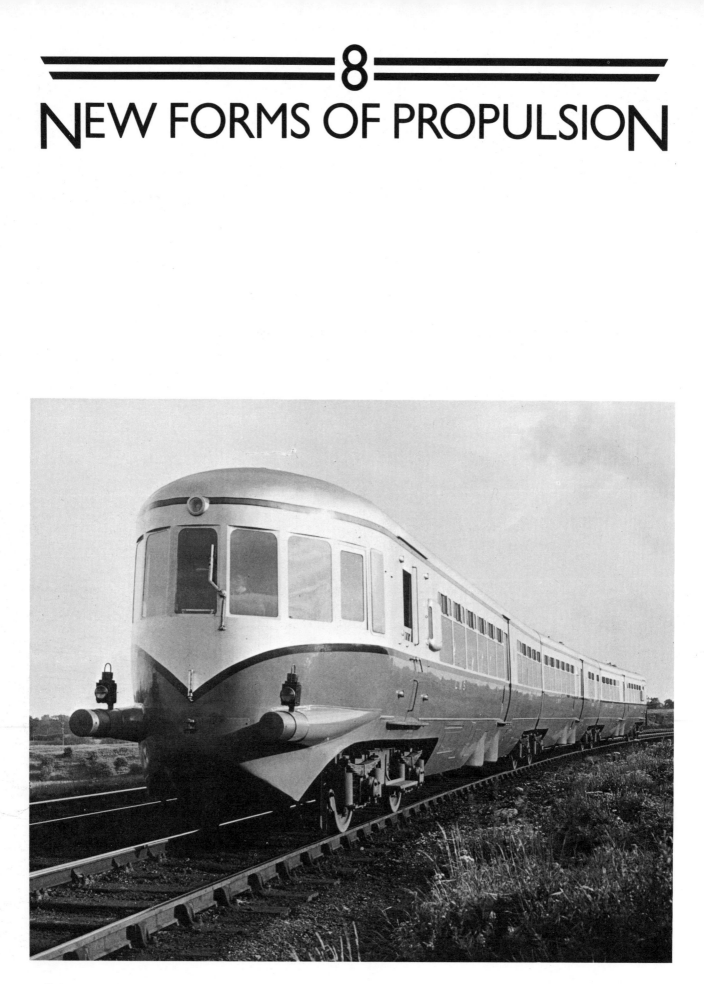

left:
The three-car diesel multiple-unit train designed for the LMS in 1939. (R G Jarvis)

A British Rail standard class 9F 2–10–0 No 92155 brings the empty stock of an excursion train into the platform at New Street station, Birmingham, in the summer of 1962. (A W Flowers)

Seven years after nationalisation the British Transport Commission was at last allowed by the Government to embark on a massive and very necessary re-investment programme. In 1955 it was given the go-ahead for a modernisation plan involving capital expenditure of £1240 million. Most of that money was to be used on new forms of tractive power and on modern rolling stock. At last, too, there was to be a national network of electrified lines spreading outwards from London. Electrification was scheduled for the East Coast route from Kings Cross to Doncaster, Leeds and York (possibly); for Euston to Birmingham, Liverpool and Manchester; for the Eastern Region line from Chelmsford to Ipswich taking in the Clacton, Harwich and Felixstowe branches. In addition the Kings Cross suburban system, the South Kent coast lines, the rest of Southern Region's main lines east of Reading and Portsmouth, and the Liverpool Street and north-east London suburbs were to be included in the electrification programme. Elsewhere the steam locomotives were to be phased out and replaced by diesel locomotives and multiple-unit railcars. The BTC made the proviso that if it became possible to extend electrification still further, the dieselisation programme would be cut.

There was also, under the Modernisation Plan, to be major and much-needed expenditure on reconstructing the tracks which had been so well-worn during the war years and now had to be brought up to higher standards, on resignalling and on re-organisation of the freight business. More than one-quarter of the total investment capital was intended for the restructuring and modernisation of this important sector of the railway industry and most of the money was scheduled to go on new wagons, new or modernised marshalling yards and – at long last – on equipping all wagons with continuous brake systems. Regrettably, the Transport Commission failed totally to take note of overseas experience and instead of opting for the efficient compressed air brake system, decided to continue with the vacuum brake which, as stated earlier, had been fitted to a small proportion of goods vehicles before nationalisation. It was a decision which was to prove extraordinarily costly: in less than ten years a change of policy made compressed-air braking standard for all new rolling stock so that thousands of new passenger and freight vehicles built with vacuum brakes in the meantime were obsolescent. Even more serious was the fact that new locomotives had been equipped with the now out-of-date system and were particularly costly to modify for air braking. Such was the cost of this serious error of judgment that even by the late 1970s, though all inter-city front-rank services were modernised with air braking, thousands of other vehicles (both passenger and freight) were still either vacuum braked or had no continuous braking system.

The Plan was defective on other serious matters, particularly in the way it naively ignored the general economic state of the country which had considerable implications on the execution of the Plan and had a direct effect on the changing traffic patterns and rising costs. Its authors apparently could see no reason to reduce the size of the country's railway system or its operation and seemed to think that the panacea was to speed up services by using diesel or electric locomotives and installing electrically controlled colour-light signalling. Other 'cures' were to be the improved tracks, modern stations and new depots. At this stage, nobody thought to question whether all parts of the system were suitable for modernisation or even whether they were still needed.

Within three years the Plan was being re-appraised. Already the

The year 1967 saw the end of express operation by steam – the Bournemouth line out of Waterloo. This picture, taken in June 1967, some two months before the end, shows Bournemouth shed with diesel and steam power just prior to third-rail electrification. (P B Whitehouse)

railways were running at an operating loss, costs were rising rapidly and freight traffic levels did not, because of upsets in industry, relate to forecasts. Problems were also growing on the re-equipment front. Before it was abolished, the Railway Executive had intended to carry out a thorough evaluation of 174 diesel locomotives in three broad power ranges. These were to have been grouped around selected depots and their individual records of performance, operating and maintenance costs studied closely so that each could be assessed as to potential for mass-production. The need for this somewhat tentative approach was because BR and the groups of pre-nationalisation days lacked diesel experience, though there were the five main-line diesels evolved by the LMS and SR in the background.

These five apart, British diesel locomotive manufacture had been mainly in the form of limited, custom-built orders for overseas railways. The diesel types for this market were not considered to be readily adaptable to BR traffic requirements. Though the American railroads had wide experience of diesels and the United States could offer a well-tried diesel locomotive industry, political pressure in Britain prevented advantage being taken of this obvious solution to BRs problems. British diesel manufacturers were crying out for the opportunity to get in on the market so that they could gain experience of main-line diesel locomotive construction and turn it to advantage in breaking into the overseas market. Several diesel manufacturers, incidentally, were descended directly or through mergers and acquisitions, from pioneer steam locomotive builders: English Electric, for example, included among its constituent companies Robert Stephenson & Company.

The Western Region, which since nationalisation had striven to retain a degree of independence, eventually persuaded the BTC to allow it to build German-patterned diesel-hydraulic locomotives under licence. Thus it was that the first Western Region main-line diesels presented a dramatic contrast to the diesels seen elsewhere on BR. The management of the Western had been impressed by the

The LMSR 'Ro-Railer' was an experimental vehicle which on reaching the rail-head changed from its flanged wheels to tyred wheels and proceeded to its destination by road. It is seen here under test on the Harpenden-Hemel Hempstead branch in the early 1930s. (C J Allen collection)

way in which German diesel manufacturers had achieved a successful combination of fast-running engines with hydraulic transmisssions and comparatively low all-up weight, to achieve a 2000 horsepower locomotive weighing just under 80 tons. This compared with the 130-or-more tons of the diesel-electric locomotives which BR was considering. The German design was modified to meet the more restricted BR loading gauge and production began, with engines and transmission initially being imported from Germany.

Here it should be explained that there are basically three types of transmission for the power produced by a diesel engine: mechanical, through a fluid coupling, gearbox and final drive; electrical, with the engine driving an electric generator to provide current for electric traction motors; and hydraulic, through one or more torque convertors, with a fluid coupling between the drive and the driven mechanism. Electric transmission had the longest record of service and had been adopted by American railroads in the 1930s. They were the most attractive proposition to BR Regions which had electric lines because there already existed workshops to maintain electric traction equipment.

The trials of the 174 various diesel locomotives were never completed because, faced with a rapidly deteriorating financial situation,

The Great Western Railway
introduced these streamlined railcars
during the 1930s to act as branch-
line units and also (for example on
the Birmingham to Cardiff run) to
form a fast and compact inter-city
service. (P B Whitehouse)

left:
A–1–A–A–1–A No 18000, designed
in 1949 by Brown Boveri
(Switzerland) for the Western
Region, heads an express out of
Paddington. This was one of two
gas turbine locomotives built for
that Region – the experiment was
not a success. (Eric Treacy)

Dieselisation made its first impact when DMU sets began to replace steam suburban trains on the BR system. Here in 1961 the 1.15 pm (13.15) Wellington (Salop) to Lapworth train waits to leave Birmingham's Snow Hill station. This station is now closed, the tracks torn up and buildings demolished but plans are in hand under 'modern thinking' to re-open it! (M Mensing)

the BTC decided it must scrap steam and go straight into a programme of rapid dieselisation. The Commission was also faced, in reaching its decision, with a growing shortage and rising price of good steam coal and with the difficulty of recruiting good footplate and maintenance staff prepared to work in the dirty conditions which inevitably surrounded steam locomotion.

In the rush to dieselisation the BTC placed orders in 1957 for the mass production of several diesel types – in some cases prototypes had not even been completed. Such was the speed at which the BTC wanted to carry through its programme of dieselisation that in five years from the end of 1958 to 1963 the BR stable of motive power completely altered in make-up. At the beginning of that period BR had 16,108 steam locomotives, 105 main-line diesels and 2417 multiple-unit railcars. In 1963 the picture had altered so that there were only 7050 steam locomotives left while the number of main-line diesels had risen to 2051, diesel railcars numbered 4145 and shunters, 2009.

Attempting to catch up with most of the rest of the world, BR inevitably encountered many shocks and problems because it was making a changeover which was without precedent in its scale. There were many difficulties from a variety of causes, including an initial lack of purpose-built maintenance depots and fully trained staff, a failure to appreciate the need for mass production of components to be carried out in scrupulously clean conditions and to high tolerances, and the realisation that the 2000–2500hp diesel-electric locomotives with 14- or 15-coach loads were not, after all, going to bring any dramatic reductions in the journey times which steam traction had established.

The 1955 Plan had proposed the electrification of 200 miles of the East and West Coast main lines from London to the north by 1970.

Another Western Region experiment, this time successful, was the use of diesel hydraulic locomotives. D1067 *Western Druid* is shown here at Bristol Temple Meads. (Eric Treacy)

above right:
A 'Hanks' 0–6–0 diesel shunter is built at Swindon works towards the end of the 1950s. Note the steam locomotive-type chimney to make it look more respectable. (P B Whitehouse)

It was quickly realised that this was a target beyond the capabilities of the industry and of BR's electrical engineering resources. Main-line electrification from Kings Cross was therefore shelved. Electri-fication was not new and the first English electric railway had been opened by Magnus Volk in Brighton in 1883. The North Eastern and the Lancashire & Yorkshire Railways were the first main-line companies to use this form of power in 1904 in Newcastle and Liverpool. The pioneer deep-level tube railway in London had opened in the 1890s and was followed by extensions and new lines at the beginning of the twentieth century. The early electric schemes used direct current at 600–650 volts, the supply being fed through conductor rails outside the running rails. Some systems had a single conductor rail which carried the positive current with the return supply through the running rails at earth potential; others had a fourth insulated rail in the middle of the track to carry the return supply. The pioneer London Underground lines had electric loco-motives but the main-line companies worked their electric suburban services with motor coaches which were capable of being controlled as a complete unit from the leading cab. Thus was born the multiple-unit system.

It was the Midland Railway which, in 1908 and 1909, introduced alternating current on its lines between Lancaster, Morecambe and Heysham. The 6600-volt current was collected from an overhead wire and the supply transformed to a lower voltage in the motor coaches before being fed to the traction motors. On the Continent and in the United States high-voltage alternating current was being developed at the same time but successful traction by alternating current motors could only be achieved with frequencies below the standard 50 cycles per second (now referred to as 50 Hertz or 50 Hz), so the Midland generated its own supply at 25 Hz. The debate on the relative advantages of AC or DC supply for electric traction has continued ever since.

In 1909 the London, Brighton & South Coast Railway opened its AC electrification system on its line between London Bridge and Victoria, thereby responding to the competition of the tramways. This line used 6700 volts AC at 25 Hz from an overhead line. The system was extended to Coulsdon on the Brighton line, and Sutton on the Dorking and Horsham line, by 1928. Meanwhile the LNWR inaugurated conductor electrification at 630 volts DC in 1914 on its Willesden–Earls Court branch. This was the first stage of the company's conversion of suburban lines between Broad Street, Euston and Watford. The London & South Western followed a year later with 660-volt DC, third-rail electrification on suburban lines from Waterloo, an event which was later to be of importance for railways in Southern England. Also in 1915 the North Eastern introduced electric working on the Shildon–Newport line in County Durham. The NER adopted 1500 volts DC with overhead collection and trains were hauled by locomotives of the double-bogie type with traction motors mounted on the axles. (Today they would be described as having a Bo-Bo wheel arrangement on the basis that 'A' stands for one driving axle of a group, 'B' means two, etc, and that the suffix 'o' denotes independent motors on each axle.)

With the variety of electrification systems in use after World War I, standardisation was desirable and direct current seemed to be favoured. After Grouping, Herbert Walker, who had been General Manager of the LSWR and took up the same post for the Southern, brought in a 660-volt DC third-rail system as standard for the SR. By 1930

The LNWR four-rail suburban electrification of 1914 was extended in 1922 for working over district lines. Two of the three-car sets of open saloons with corridor connections wait at Richmond Station in LMS livery in 1925. (H G W Household)

Early overhead suburban electrification – the London & Brighton, South Coast EMU train in Victoria Station. (C J Allen collection)

The third-rail electrified system out of London's southern terminii was developed during the inter-war years into one of the world's most intensively used suburban systems. Here is an early EMU near Bromley in 1938. (H C Casserley)

Electric Pullman: One of Britain's best-known trains was the old 'Southern Belle' renamed 'Brighton Belle' – an all electric Pullman express with luxury now superceded by expediency. Here the 'Belle' enters Brighton in 1948. (P M Alexander)

Diesel hydraulic locomotive No D1006 *Western Stalwart* arrives at Paddington station in 1973. This class is now extinct though some have been preserved. (B N Arnold)

The ubiquitous 9Fs. Probably the most successful of all the BR standard locomotive was the 9F 2–10–0. These engines were in use all over the system and were even, at times (and strangely enough particularly on the Western Region), used on passenger trains.

No 92135 moves slowly up to the starting signal at Westerleigh yards, Gloucestershire, before joining the main line with a north-bound freight. (G F Heiron)

the company had virtually completed its electrification schemes in the London suburban area and with nearly 900 track-miles was able to claim 'the world's greatest suburban electrification'. Then came plans to extend electrification to the South Coast, starting with Brighton and Worthing. This was regarded as an extended suburban electrification scheme rather than a main-line one, and the 660-volt DC system was therefore retained. The work was completed by the end of December 1932. All services ran with multiple-unit stock, the Brighton non-stop trains being formed from six-car units, each with a Pullman car. The Southern boasted the only electric multiple-unit Pullman trains in the world and the Pullman Car Company built three five-car all-Pullman sets for the famous 'Southern Belle' service. The 'Belle' continued until 30 April 1972.

The Southern continued to extend its electrification by turning to the former LBSCR lines between 1933 and 1938 and at the same time converting other sections. In the east of its territory the supply reached Sevenoaks in 1935 and the Medway towns in 1939; the route from Waterloo to Portsmouth Harbour was completely electrified by July 1937; and on New Year's Day 1939 the Waterloo–Reading and Guildford via Ascot services began electric working. The Southern's concentration on electrification made its service popular with the commuting public in its territory. Though the topography of the area made dramatic improvements in journey times impossible, the company provided regular services at standardised departure times. The London–Brighton non-stop trains, for example, were then advertised as 'on the hour in the hour' (the 55-minute schedule came later). Such a service proved a better

New Street station, Birmingham during the chaotic period of rebuilding in the 1960s. (Colourviews Picture Library)

selling point than crack named trains and set the pattern for today's high-speed Inter-City services.

Elsewhere the first new electrification scheme to be completed after the Pringle Report – the report of one of several committees set up to recommend standards of electrification – was that for the Manchester South Junction and Altrincham joint line of 1927 which used 1500 volts DC with overhead contact wires. It was the first passenger-carrying line to use this voltage which was later accepted as standard for main-line electrification in Britain (except on the Southern) until BR changed to 25,000 AC at 50 Hz in 1956. Although the NER had planned in 1919 to electrify the York–Newcastle line on the 1500-volt DC overhead system and actually built a 4–6–4 (2–C–2 in today's classification) electric locomotive, the project was abandoned with the approach of Grouping. In the following decade the LNER drew up plans for the electrification of the Manchester–Sheffield–Wath line including a new Woodhead Tunnel through the Pennines and actually started work. Another scheme envisaged electrification of the suburban lines between Liverpool Street and Shenfield. Both schemes were on the 1500-volt DC system. Progress was interrupted by World War II but the Shenfield scheme was eventually completed by BR in 1949 and the Manchester–Sheffield–Wath in 1954.

It was against this background that in 1951 the BTC reaffirmed its faith in the 1500-volt DC overhead wire system and authorised extensions to the Liverpool Street–Shenfield scheme to Chelmsford and Southend. Even so, the Commission had been impressed by the findings of yet another committee set up to survey world develop-

The Isle of Wight once supported three independent railway systems which were grouped into one on the formation of the Southern Railway in 1923. Much of the system remained intact during early BR days but now only one line – Ryde to Sandown – exists – worked by three-rail electric trains, ex-London Transport. In happier times this ex-LSWR Adams 0–4–4T of class 02 takes water at Ventnor town. (G D King)

ment of electric traction and it ordered a trial conversion of the Lancaster–Morecambe–Heysham line to high-voltage AC electrification using the 50 Hz industrial supply frequency. The French also carried out main-line trials of this system and by the mid-1950s had found it so successful in terms of economical running, of installation costs and of providing excellent traction, that the BTC this time took note of overseas experience and adopted the 25,000-volt (25kV) 50 Hz supply for all future electrification. The only exception, as we have mentioned, was the Southern Region, which retained the third-rail system, though increasing the supply from 660 volts to 750 volts DC when equipment renewals were due. This system was so widely used in the region that it would not have made economic sense to attempt conversion.

On the London–Midland, AC electrification continued with the completion of the Manchester–Crewe section in September 1960. The system was gradually extended in the region, first from Liverpool to Crewe and then south to Nuneaton. It eventually reached Euston in 1966. A year later lines in the Birmingham area and from Rugby to Stafford were added and by 1974 the whole of the West Coast route north of Crewe to Glasgow, over Shap at Beattock had been converted. Suburban schemes such as those around Glasgow and in the north and east of London from Liverpool Street (including the main line to Clacton) and Fenchurch Street to Southend, were also changed over. Some inner suburban lines were at first supplied with 6250 volts, the trains being converted to work on this lower voltage as well as the full 25,000 volts. Automatic equipment was installed so that the voltage changeover was initiated at the boundary between the two supplies. It was thought at first that the 25 kV system required at least an 11-inch clearance above and below the contact wire to

Oliver Bulleid's Southern Region 0–6–6–0 Leader class experimental locomotive performs on trial. This class never entered regular service. (Cecil J Allen collection)

avoid flashovers and this would have required the rebuilding of hundreds of bridges. The lower voltage obviated much of this reconstruction work. In fact it was later found that 11-inches was over-cautious and clearances were reduced. At the same time the go-ahead was given to abandon the lower voltage in future. To give full compatability, the lines from Liverpool Street which were originally electrified at 1500 volts DC were converted to AC in readiness for electrification extensions on high voltage alternating current. All these electrification schemes and some non-electric trunk routes were completely resignalled with colour-light signals and, in most cases, control from centralised power signalboxes which are in charge of long lengths of line.

British Rail's alternating current electrification schemes were not without problems. Soon after the commissioning of the Manchester–Crewe section in 1960 massive rises in construction costs so frightened Parliament that the project was stopped while the finances were examined. The problems lay not only in inflation but also in all the extras, like station rebuilding, which were not essentials of electrification but had been thrown in as part of the overall scheme. Additionally, there had been little real appreciation of the savings which electrification could bring by way of track simplification; much of the conversion was carried out on the basis of what was already there, rather than on what was really needed. There were also major equipment faults which brought the Glasgow scheme and those in north and east London to a halt and took many months to sort out.

In the diesel field, too, it was not until the mid-1960s that the results of the rush to dieselisation were unravelled and some order and a greater measure of reliability were obtained. Prototype diesel locomotives which had been brought in without proper trials were

London–Paris and London–Brussels Wagons Lits night ferry service. Photograph shows sleeping cars going on board one of the ferries at Dover. (Colourviews Picture Library)

replaced and new construction was standardised on single diesel-electric designs in each of four power ranges. Meantime the Western Region had succeeded in maintaining its independent air and had expanded its diesel-hydraulic main-line fleet to four types. Of these the most imposing and largest was the 2700hp class 52 Western. The region all the time faced strong opposition from BR's chiefs and from industry because of the German involvement. Finally, in the face of claims against their high initial and maintenance costs and allegedly chronic failure records, the diesel-hydraulics were condemned by the railway hierarchy in favour of locomotives with diesel-electric transmission. These were, it was insisted, more robust and capable of sustaining medium high speed at lesser cost. BR headquarters ordered the end of diesel-hydraulic construction and the conversion of the Western to diesel-electric. Completion of the total elimination of the hydraulic version took 15 years.

The new standard high-powered diesel-electric was the class 47 with six powered axles. Introduced as a 2750hp, 95mph locomotive weighing 114 tons, the unit was found to be subject to stresses and had to be derated to 2580hp. Only 22 British Railways engines existed until the mid-1960s which were capable of fulfilling the inter-city speed estimates contained in the 1955 Plan. They were the 3300hp class 55 Deltics made by English Electric which were so named because the company had designed them round the delta-shaped 18-cylinder, opposed-piston Napier engine which had originally been developed for high-speed naval craft. English Electric had constructed a prototype speculatively and demonstrated its

'Hengist' is used on the Dover/Folkstone–Calais Sealink ferry service. (British Railways)

capabilities of speed and power – which were almost of electric-style proportions – on BR main-lines in 1959. The BTC then agreed that the East Coast route should have a fleet of the Deltics to compensate for its frustrated hope of electrification. However, there were possible weaknesses about the proposals to introduce the Deltic in terms of its high initial cost and its complexity; there were also objections to the fact that the BTC was resorting to an engine which had previously been untried on rail. Because of these objections the Deltic was brought into service under a contract which provided that English Electric maintained the engines, largely on the basis of a pool of replacement spare assemblies. The Deltics on the East Coast route, and the LMR electric locomotives were the leaders of British Rail's express services which were introduced in the late 1960s under the name 'Inter-City' with well-publicised daily 100mph speeds over suitable sections of track.

Even in the first half of the 1960s there was alarm at the mounting BR losses. The politicians stepped in and a committee – the Stedeford Committee, after its Chairman, Sir Ivan Stedeford – was set up to examine the future role of railways and how they were to be financed and administered. A member of that committee was Dr Richard Beeching, who was then technical director of Imperial Chemical Industries (ICI). The Transport Act 1963 paved the way for the British Railways Board which had been recommended by the Stedeford Committee. Dr Beeching was appointed first Chairman of the Board and was to write his name into railway history.

Brought in at the end of the 1950s to rationalise the railway system. Dr Richard (now Lord) Beeching, once of ICI, set about his task with considerable thoroughness. The present track mileage is almost unchanged from the final wielding of his axe. (John Adams)

The new British Railways Board and its chairman, Dr Beeching, took a searching look at the railways system under its control and soon appreciated that widespread changes were needed. Beeching found that about half the system carried roughly 95 per cent of traffic, while the other half carried the remainder. With local bus routes then able to serve most rural areas more efficiently than railways and with the great increase in private car ownership since the end of the war, many lines which were lossmakers clearly had to be closed and small intermediate stations on main lines were shut.

Closures of unremunerative services were not new. Some went in World War I, others in the 1930s, and BR had gradually accelerated closures in the 1950s. But none of this had the widespread effects of the sweep of the axe which was to follow the Beeching examination. As chief author of the *Reshaping Report* issued by the British Railways Board, Beeching lopped branches, cross-country lines and even one or two main lines. Among major casualties were the Midland & Great Northern and Somerset & Dorset joint lines and the Great Central London extension main line, opened as recently as 1899. Gone too were the North British main line from Carlisle to Edinburgh, the Midland main line from Derby to Manchester and the original Midland Counties line from Rugby to Leicester which was part of the first route from Euston to the North East.

On the traffic side, local stopping passenger trains ceased on many routes as there were no local stations left for them to serve. The greatest changes were made on the freight side. Beeching was convinced that the principal role of the railway was as a bulk carrier and that freight should be organised on a trainload rather than a wagonload basis.

The handling of small consignments of packages and crates was one of the biggest lossmakers and since road transport was involved at some stage of almost every freight operation it was thought that small consignments would be best left to the road transport industry, collecting and delivering from centrally placed sundries depots, with trunk rail haulage in trainloads between depots far apart. Other freight was to be carried in containers, with road collection and delivery at the start and finish of the journey and high-speed, long-distance rail haulage in between in special 75mph freightliner container trains. Coal for power stations was carried by block trains of hopper wagons designed to be loaded at pitheads and unloaded automatically at the destination as they continued to move slowly. In this way two or three trains could be handled in a working day, providing a service which was virtually non-stop. Indeed, they soon acquired the name-tag 'merry-go-round trains' and presented a great contrast to the days just passed when wagons spent much time being sorted in marshalling yards and waiting to be loaded or unloaded. Domestic coal movement was re-organised to run as block loads to centralised coal distribution depots; other bulk traffic carried in block trains included oil, chemicals, fertilizer, aggregates and car components.

The effect of running so much traffic as through traffic from one originating point to a single destination was to reduce dramatically the number of trains needing to be remarshalled, and in turn reduce the use of many marshalling yards, some of which had been built or

left:
Edinburgh Waverley station with type 5 D/E Deltic No 9018 *Ballymoss* at the head of the up 'Flying Scotsman'. (Eric Treacy)

Type 5 class 55 Deltic No 55–009 as D9099 *Alycidon* with a down express arrives at York. (Eric Treacy)

enlarged only a few years before. Many became 'white elephants', as did such structures as the flyover at Bletchley, which had been built in the 1960s to carry freight trains over the electrified West Coast main line on to a planned new ring route avoiding London – a route which, in the event was no longer necessary.

Another more positive feature of the new regime was the introduction of new high-capacity wagons, among them long-wheelbase four-wheel vans of up to 45 tons capacity (fully loaded) and massive bogie tank wagons with a loaded weight of 1000 tons. All were fully equipped with power brakes and capable of running at speeds of 60–75mph.

Since the mid-1960s successive governments had been far more involved in the way British Railways had been run because of the financial losses which were being incurred despite closures of uneconomic lines and more progressive modernisation of the remainder.

The hour is coming up to 17.55 at Paddington, – departure time for the Carmarthen-bound 'Red Dragon' standing at platform 5. The engine would have been either a four-cylinder Castle class 4–6–0 or a two-cylinder standard Britannia Pacific. (G F Heiron)

View of New Street station, Birmingham, taken in 1962 showing a south-bound express waiting to depart from platform 3. This view gives a clear indication of the umbrella roofing which spanned the construction period between the overall glass roof and the new station now in use. (Colourviews Picture Library)

Closures were not always the answer, for lossmaking services carried valuable traffic as feeders to otherwise profitable main lines, while many suburban services around cities – Southern electric services around London, for example – fulfilled essential social needs. The principal of grant payments by Government or local authorities was accepted to support essential passenger services which were lossmaking. Moreover, the Government through the Department of Transport and the Treasury, has had to approve and give financial assistance for new works such as the new electrification schemes, resignalling programmes, large purchases of new locomotives and rolling stock, and research.

It was against all the upheavals of the Beeching era, with a slimmer system getting to grips with new operating methods, that British Rail faced the 1970s. Steam traction had finally come to an end in regular service in 1968 and diesel and electric traction were emerging from their rather troubled starts. Not all of the Beeching period had been negative and demoralising. Some proposals were highly positive, as, for example, the faster more frequent passenger services and the better outlook for bulk freight by rail. Overall policy control by the politicians had come to stay though, whichever Government was in power and whatever its political views on transport. Indeed, the 1970s, despite frustration arising from the economic state of the country as a whole, were to prove as exciting for rail transport in Britain as the first railways had been 150 years before. A growing energy crisis, in which oil shortages were becoming serious and were accompanied by ever-increasing prices, was beginning to show the economic advantages of rail over road transport. Further large-scale electrification schemes looked financially more attractive in such a context.

By the end of the 1960s, too, it was clear that the London Midland Region's electric East Coast Deltic services with 100mph top speeds and average speeds of 80mph (compared with 60mph by steam in the late 1950s) and frequent internal services were succeeding in the battle for passengers against private cars on the new motorway network and airlines. Indeed, the commercial success of LMR electric and East Coast Deltic services soon brought calls from other routes for equipment capable of 100mph-plus maximum speeds and end-to-end averages of 80mph or more.

A container is being transferred at a freightliner terminal. Lorries collect and deliver the containers locally, leaving the trunk haul to rail. (British Railways)

Improvements to track and signalling technology made possible at relatively small cost some improvements in services by eliminating features which had necessitated speed restrictions on some stretches. The East Coast main line was brought up to the standard required for continuous 100mph running, practically from London to Doncaster and for 85 miles of the remaining 112 to Newcastle. This was achieved by the Eastern Region in the early 1970s for an outlay of about £60 million and in 1976 it was possible for the 'Flying Scotsman' to improve its Kings Cross-Edinburgh timing to 5 hours 27 minutes, an average of 72.1mph and a best recorded route schedule of 80.8mph.

In the spring of 1974 the completion of the electrification of the West Coast main line from north of Crewe to Glasgow meant that the great climbs to the fells of the North of England and Scotland were reduced to comparatively minor pulls by the power of the locomotives. Shap and Beattock banks, with inclines of 1-in-74.5, which had tested the steam locomotives, now had the 'Royal Scot' roaring over them as it ran from London to Glasgow at an average speed of 80.3mph in a five-hour journey (including an intermediate stop at Preston). One result was that by the autumn of 1974 the route had carried over 50 per cent more passengers than in 1973. Improvements in timings continued on all regions and in 1978 the

Permanent relaying with concrete sleepers at Hest Bank on the LM Region meets the increased and faster traffic on electrification. (Colourviews Picture Library)

Electric locomotives at Crewe station. The new 25,000-volt AC overhead system on the up-to-date West Coast main line has now been extended from London (Euston) to Birmingham, Manchester, Liverpool and Glasgow. (Eric Treacy)

Until very recent times all signal boxes on the British Railway system were worked by signalmen working shifts and using interlocked manual lever frames with electric block instruments. Here is a signal box on the LMS Railway at Carlisle showing levers, block instruments and a track circuit diagram. (Colourviews Picture Library)

A multi-aspect colour-light signal. (Colourviews Picture Library)

LMR electric main line carried 165 trains daily with start-to-stop averages of 80mph or more, with a top of 88.8mph between Rugby and Watford Junction. In 1939 the whole British Railway network had 116 daily runs timed at an average of 60mph under steam.

British Rail discovered, as the SR had before, that regular-interval, or repeat-pattern train services were justified and economically viable. The public was offered more trains each day because the regular timetable structure made programming of men and equipment simpler and involved rapid turnrounds of locomotives, train-sets and crews at the terminals. The regular-interval train timetables also resulted in a completely different attitude by the railway management to the way in which train-sets could be used. It was recognised that there was no practicality in making up a standard train formation for a specific route to use it at only specific times, such as rush-hours. This had been the practice for many years, with train-sets made up to suit peak morning and evening rush-hour standing idle for the rest of the day. Other trains, for use in the middle of the day might make one journey only during the day and be used again the following day for the return trip; while that return trip was being made another set had to cover the original 'outward' journey. The policy of turning round as many train-sets as possible in the platform obviated this duplication and saved on manhours and operating costs. Standard train formations could receive essential basic servicing as they stood in the platform after discharging one load of passengers and before taking on the next. The highest possible average mileage per day helped to cut the total requirement for the coaching stock fleet.

The system demanded that the train must be made up as the best possible compromise in terms of the accommodation which would be needed on different routes at different times of the day. High utilisation could often only be achieved by complicated rostering which brought a set of coaches into a station on one route and sent it out on a completely different one. It might not return to its original

With modernisation, the older forms of train control, *viz* manual signal boxes and semaphore signals, gave way, in most instances, to the electric power box controlling a large area of a Division and the replacement of the once-common signal post with its red and yellow semaphore arms with multi-aspect colour lights.

above:
Wilmslow power box on the Manchester line of the London Midland Region. (British Railways)

above right:
Watford Junction power signal box showing illuminated track diagram and control panel. (BR LM Region)

point of departure for 48 hours, having covered several routes in the meantime. In compensation, the peak travel hours tended to be eased by the greater frequency of trains and by the incentive of reduced fares for off-peak travel.

Success of the system spurred BR into planning even faster trains and all-round improvements in passenger comfort. The original standard BR passenger coaches of the 1950s had introduced such features as all-steel construction and greater safety but the layout, seat design and decor had not advanced greatly for 25 years. Moreover, at speeds of more than 70mph the standard BR coach was noisy and hardly the best ride. In the mid-1960s a BR Mark II version appeared with new-style bogies which owed something to Continental practice. It rode fairly steadily up to 100mph and had a brighter interior, new seat designs and modern decor. Second-class coaches (third-class had been renamed second throughout most of Western Europe in 1956) were entirely of the open saloon type and the side-corridor compartment style was on its way out. Succeeding batches of Mark II coaches had improvements in detail including a change from vacuum to compressed-air braking. The fourth version, MkIID of 1972, was equipped with full air-conditioning and dispensed with opening windows in passenger saloons.

Air-conditioning had been used in five sets of diesel-electric Pullman multiple units in the early 1960s built primarily to attract the first-class business market. Known as the 'Blue Pullmans' for their blue-and-white livery in place of the traditional brown-and-cream, they were fixed-formation trains with a diesel-electric streamlined power car at each end which included passenger accommodation. There were kitchen and parlour cars between. Three eight-car sets for the Western Region included a small amount of second-class accommodation but the two six-car units used for the St Pancras–Manchester Midland Pullman were entirely first-class. Like all Pullmans on BR they were entirely owned by the railway. A sup-

The mid-1960s found the main West Coast route from London to Birmingham, Manchester, Liverpool and Glasgow electrified by the 25,000-volt AC overhead system giving a frequency of service hitherto unrealized. A Manchester express about to depart from London (Euston) behind AL6 class electric locomotive No E3141. (Eric Treacy)

plementary fare was charged on top of the ordinary fare. The cars were effectively sound-proofed and with modern decor and ergonomically designed seats they were far above the standards of ordinary BR trains and equal to the best in Europe. The 'Blue Pullmans' were intended to provide a luxury service at fairly high speeds – they were designed for 90mph top speeds – on routes paralleling the LMR West Coast route during disruption caused by electrification work. From 1967 all five sets were allocated to the Western Region for service between London and South Wales or the Midlands. Pullman services were on the way out for with improvements to ordinary standards they no longer offered so great an incentive in terms of improved comfort. The Southern Region finally abandoned Pullmans in 1972 and its South Coast services were given the role of being little more than outer-suburban in character. The 'Blue Pullmans' were withdrawn in 1973.

They had established the principle of a fixed-formation train with self-contained power cars needing no terminal locomotive movements and hence capable of quick turnrounds in the platform with servicing and kitchen restocking taking place at the same time. Similar advantages of quick turnrounds were achieved on the Glasgow–Edinburgh service in the early 1970s with fixed formation sets of coaches by two diesel locomotives, one at each end, and with multiple-unit control of both from the leading cab. They thus had all the flexibility of the lighter lower-powered diesel multiple-unit trains used on local services.

While all this was going on BR started research in the 1960s into new-generation trains going beyond the then known rail technology.

An EMU leaves Birmingham New Street with a slow train. (British Railways Board LM Region)

Apart from a scientific approach to problems of wheel behaviour on rail at high speeds, research began into the concept of an Advanced Passenger Train, or APT, which, it was claimed would ride satisfactorily at up to 155mph on the straight and would be able to take curves 40 per cent faster than conventional trains without the need for modifications to existing main-line routes.

Aerospace research played an important part in the design theory of the APT, in which it was proposed that a lightweight coach built using aerospace techniques, should embody a patent suspension system that enabled the wheels to steer round curved track as the coach body tilted automatically to the correct angle. The body-tilting system counteracted excessive effects of centrifugal force at high speed which might have upset passengers. In 1967, when the project was unveiled, the British Railways Board optimistically announced that, if sufficient resources were made available to complete research and development, the first APTs could be running in service by 1972. Government money was made available in 1968 to meet half the estimated research and development cost but by 1972, when the first prototype APT took to the rails there had been some radical changes in design. In the meantime the railways were again, like the whole country, having financial problems and the Government was reluctant to put more money into a technology which was so far unproven.

Traditionalists in BR mechanical engineering felt that conventional trains still had greater potential and with commercial calls for more positive improvements the BRB agreed in 1970 to order a fresh development of the orthodox design in the form of the 125mph

High-Speed Diesel Train or HST. When it emerged in 1972 the prototype proved to be a double-ended set of seven new Mk III coaches (at 75ft, longer than previous types) with a pair of 2500hp diesel-electric power cars. At almost the same time the prototype APT was unveiled: a four-car gas turbine-electric powered set.

Both prototype trains went on to set new British speed records during their trials. The HST reached 143mph on almost level track between Darlington and York on 11 June 1973; the APT touched 151mph between Reading and Swindon in August 1975.

Approval for mass production was given first to the HST and the initial batch went into service on the Western Region's Paddington–Bristol/South Wales routes in October 1976, after track and signalling improvements had been made to nearly 100 miles of route. Introduction of the service involved the setting of new 125mph standards for equipment and precise timetabling. The resulting passenger service was equalled only by the famous Japanese New Tokaido Line for end-to-end speed and frequency. Significantly, the Japanese results are achieved on brand-new lines designed for and used by electric passenger trains whereas the Western Region's BR Inter-City 125 operation involves fitting in 48 125mph diesel trains each weekday with the existing traffic of an established railway service. City-to-city start-to-stop average speeds are recorded of over 93mph between London and Newport and the exceptional acceleration of the HSTs produces short sprints timed at a peak

The High Speed Train with its 125mph rating has revolutionised traffic on the Western route to Bristol and on the East Coast main line. These services, introduced in 1976, comprise two power cars each containing a 2250hp diesel engine and seven coaches including catering vehicles – all air conditioned. Here HST 254.017 stands at Kings Cross station, London, with the 1600 hours 'Talisman' for Edinburgh.

Dining on British Rail's High Speed Train. (G Freeman Allen collection)

Not yet in service, British Rail's experimental Advanced Passenger Train became the fastest train ever to run in Britain on 10 August 1977 when it ran at 152mph during trials on a 20-mile section of the Bristol to London main line between Swindon and Reading on the Western Region. (British Railways Board)

Torbay Steam Railway – 64XX
0–6–0PT No 6412 waits to leave
Kingswear with an afternoon train
for Paignton. The Dart Valley
Railway is one of Britain's leading
tourist lines. Sold by BR to its new
owners, it was officially re-opened
by Dr (now Lord) Beeching. (Brian
Stephenson)

average of 103.3mph. The new service brought Bristol closer to
London in travelling time than many outer suburban stations in the
Southern Region and one result was that passenger carryings on the
Western HST routes rose by one-third in the first two years of the
Inter-City 125.

The second series of HSTs, including eight intermediate coaches,
opened up a new service on the East Coast route in 1978. The 'Flying
Scotsman's' time for the London–Edinburgh journey was cut to
4 hours 52 minutes, with an average of 87.7mph to the first stop at
Newcastle. That timing was further improved after the full allocation
of HSTs had been delivered. Then more high-speed services could
be operated, simplifying timetabling, and the 'Scotsman's' schedule
was dropped to 4½ hours. Further extensions of the use of HSTs
came in 1979 when they were introduced on the London–Plymouth

With steam now gone from the main-line railway, some still lingers on in preservation. In addition to the tourist-type lines some privately owned express engines operate spasmodically over BR's tracks on chartered excursions – one big problem is maintenance and the cost thereof. However some serious attempts are being made to deal with this situation. Here is the workshop of the Birmingham Railway Museum at Tyseley. (Alan Wood)

Although there were many narrow-gauge railway systems extant in England and Wales and one in Scotland, few of these fell into the hands of the main-line companies. The LMS inherited the Leek & Manifold in Derbyshire; the Southern took the Lynton & Barnstaple in Devon; the Great Western took the Welshpool & Llanfair, the Corris and the Vale of Rheidol in Wales. The latter still runs as a tourist line and is British Railways' only steam-operated section. (P B Whitehouse)

route and then to the routes linking Newcastle, Leeds, Manchester, Sheffield and Liverpool with South Wales and the West Country through Birmingham.

The evolution of the APT called a 25kV electric power unit to be used on the West Coast route from Euston. This route, with its gradients and bends, lends itself to the exploitation of the APTs power and its ability to take curves faster than an orthodox train without causing any passenger discomfort. Because it was thought necessary to gain experience of the new units before mass production was authorised, only three sets were manufactured initially for revenue-earning service. They were designated APT-P.

Each set includes two power cars and 12 trailers. They were expected to be introduced on the Euston–Glasgow run in 1980, working to existing schedules but then aiming for an average journey time of

Most of London's termini have a considerable commuter traffic but those serving the east, south-east and south bear the brunt. Here are some of the morning crowds arriving at Liverpool Street by modern electric multiple-unit trains. (Colourviews Picture Library)

4 hours 10 minutes, or 96.4mph without exceeding a maximum of 125mph. Regular 150mph operation would involve heavy investment in in-cab continuous signalling, which would be essential at that speed because drivers would be unable to rely on fleeting glimpses of intermittent lineside signals. A regular 150mph service would also necessitate expensive modifications to the electrification supply system so that a single sub-station would be capable of handling the peak power output demanded if several APTs entered its section simultaneously. These and other considerations make it unlikely at present that the APT will be in a position to take over from the HST before the mid-1980s.

The future of railways, with 150 years of history behind them, and despite political wrangling, still looks secure, the more so with a potential world oil shortage, since railways, unlike road transport, can already operate economically on electric power. Other forms of guided transport have been talked about glibly as the 'transport of the future' but at present, there is little which has so far been achieved by monorails, tracked hovercraft or guided, mechanically levitated vehicles that could not be equalled by the conventional railway at far less cost.

INDEX